Cool Mind, Warm Heart

Cool Mind, Warm Heart

How to Communicate with Body, Mind, Heart, and Soul

Robert Boyer, Ph.D.

Cool Mind, Warm Heart

How to Communicate with Body, Mind, Heart, and Soul

Robert Boyer, Ph.D.

First Edition
Library of Congress Control Number: 2008908610
ISBN: 1-4392-0906-5

©Copyright 2007 Robert Boyer, Ph.D.
All rights reserved.

No part of this book may be reproduced, captured, or stored, in any form, without written permission from the author, except for brief excerpts quoted with citation in reviews.

Published by Seven Roses, Inc., Fairfield, IA, USA 52556.
First edition 2008.
Printed in the United States of America.

It's been said that God gave us two ears and one mouth to remind us to listen twice as much as we talk.

TABLE OF CONTENTS

INTRODUCTION viii

I. BASIC PRINCIPLES OF COMMUNICATION 1

    1. Feelings, Thoughts, and Behavior..2
    2. The Cycle of Feelings, Thoughts, and Behavior 6
    3. Increasing the Positive Influence of Feelings, Thoughts, and Behavior....... 10
    4. The Flow of Feelings, Thoughts, and Behavior 14
        Putting It All Together... 18

II. BODY AND BEHAVING 20

    Attending Skills... 21
    5. Attending to Gestures.. 22
    6. Attending to Facial Expressions 26
    7. Attending to Voice.. 30
    8. Attending to Speech 34
        Putting It All Together... 38

    Engaging Skills 39
    9. Listening... 40
    10. Prompting 44
    11. Questioning 48
    12. Matching 52
        Putting It All Together... 56

    Listening Skills 57
    13. Summarizing.. 58
    14. Validating... 62
    15. Empathizing 66
        Putting It All Together... 70

    Emotion Management Skills 71
    16. Disarming 72
    17. Disengaging... 76
    18. Venting... 80
    19. Grounding.. 84
    20. Resetting 88
        Putting It All Together... 92

III. MIND AND THINKING 93

Solution Skills 95
21. Solution Orienting 96
22. Self-Talking 100
23. Reframing 104
24. Decision Making 108
25. Solution Building 112
26. Negotiating 116
27. Presenting 120
28. Leading 124
29. Teaching 128
Putting It All Together 132

IV. HEART AND FEELING 133

Empowering Skills 135
30. Asserting 136
31. Self-Disclosing 140
32. Respecting 144
33. Motivating 148
34. Empowering 152
35. Mediating 156
36. Counseling 160
37. Parenting 164
38. Partnering 168
Putting It All Together 172

V. SOUL AND BEING 173

Actualizing Skills 175
39. Integrating 176
40. Unifying 180
Putting It All Together: Summary and Conclusion 184

LIST OF COMMUNICATION SKILLS 187

REFERENCES 190

ACKNOWLEDGEMENTS AND DEDICATION 191

INTRODUCTION

Communication is simple; miscommunication is very complicated. We spend much of our lives trying to communicate, but almost no time learning how to do it. How we communicate affects us physically, emotionally, mentally, and spiritually. It directly influences body, mind, heart, and soul—in us as well as in others.

Many people feel starved for someone to listen and connect deeply with them. But all too often our attempts result in miscommunication, even when the intent was positive. Rather than understanding and acceptance, we can become closed, defensive, and stressed. The overworked executive who is rude to his assistant, the hurried doctor who virtually ignores her patients' emotions, the husband who talks sports for hours but can't talk with his wife about family matters for ten minutes, and the struggling parents who routinely yell at their children—these are examples of people who aren't communicating effectively and thereby create more stress and disharmony in our world. Today, many couples may average only a few minutes a day of healthy communication with each other, and even less with their children.

Given this state of affairs, it isn't at all surprising that our society is so conflict-ridden. Stress and tension build up from little miscommunications. And their effects accumulate, contributing to emotional and physical health problems, family tension, community problems including crime and violence, and even conflict between groups of people and nations. One important contribution to outbreaks of violence all over the world is the boiling over of stress from billions of miscommunications in our daily lives. Miscommunication results in confusion, frustration, mistrust, loneliness, and wasted time and energy that erode both our sense of self-respect and our sense of self-responsibility. But it does give us plenty to do, and we are frequently so busy dealing with the negative effects of our miscommunication that we forget the simple joys of this incredible adventure of living on Earth.

On the other hand, we love it when people communicate effectively. We feel better about ourselves as well as others, and it promotes healthier relationships, attitudes, and lifestyles. Skill in communicating isn't trying to analyze, judge, advise, manipulate, get one up on, or psych someone up or out. It is simply listening carefully, and responding in a way that encourages acceptance and understanding. Effective, healthy communicating is a powerful skill, but not a superhuman skill. It's a skill we all need and can learn with practice. This book covers all the skills necessary for you to be an effective, healthy communicator.

The book presents fundamental principles and skills of communication in user-friendly tools for the practical person, without analytic approaches that complicate the mind. It presents 36 skills covering the full range from basic to advanced skills, all of which can be used in everyday life. Designed to serve as a how to book, it is straight to the point, using simple terms and realistic examples without elaborate, time-consuming stories or explanations. It is a concise, comprehensive training guide to practical communication skills.

The skills are presented in a style that is brief, clear, and easy to reference. Each skill is described in a short four-page chapter with ten basic points. Each chapter includes a definition, a summary, and examples of ineffective and effective uses of the skill. Each sub-section of chapters ends with a brief summary—called *Putting It All Together*—which organizes the skills into the unique systematic approach to communication the book presents.

The first section of the book sets out basic principles of this new systematic approach to communication. In the following sections, the principles are applied progressively to deeper levels from outer to inner levels, corresponding to deeper levels of behavior, thinking, feeling, and being. First are skills primarily related to the outer level of body and behaving, including body language and emotional behavior. The next skills go deeper to the inner level of mind and thinking, then deeper still to the level of heart and feeling, and finally to the deepest level of soul and being. This unique systematic approach strengthens the clarity and power of communication by organizing the skills into a framework of how the levels of heart, mind, body, and behavior function more smoothly with each other. This book provides a deeper, more integrated, and more complete understanding of how to communicate than other books on this topic.

Although the book focuses on practical skills and not on theory, it is based on the most advanced research on how the mind works. The skills are drawn from contemporary psychological theories and research.[1] But they also incorporate ancient wisdom in the oldest traditions of knowledge. I have found in my research that this ancient wisdom is presented most comprehensively in modern scientific terms in the work of Vedic scientist and educator Maharishi Mahesh Yogi.[2] The book unites modern scientific knowledge with time-tested ancient wisdom in skills that are easy to learn, simple and profound.

Like many useful skills, however, they require practice. Walking is natural, but it requires practice; communication is also natural, and it takes training and practice too. Although a formal training program can be helpful, it isn't necessary in order to develop the skills. Reading and re-reading the skills, attending more carefully to how you and other people interact, and using the book for reference as you have fun practicing the skills will develop and refine them. With practice, the new skills naturally replace old, ineffective patterns. The initial awkwardness in applying the new skills fades out as the skills become second-nature with regular use.

This book isn't written to be read straight through like a novel. It is recommended that each skill be studied and applied in your daily interactions with people, as you progress through the book. The sequence of skills is designed to increase attentive sensitivity and more careful listening as the training progresses. Regular use of the skills reveals their many levels of subtlety. But deeply learning the skills identified as the most important is more useful than superficially learning them all. The skills are refined through appreciating the subtler flow of emotional and mental energy within and between people. One of the most important communication skills is careful listening. When we listen carefully, people give us useful information in subtle clues and signals. When we listen with deeply settled cool mind and warm heart, Nature whispers to us her most wonderful secrets.

The skills in this book need to be taught to our children along with language training at home and at school. It will be wonderful—and quite relieving—when our children grow up using communication skills to foster healthier relationships. The first step is to apply the skills in your own life. It will help you be a better role model, and you will get along better with your family, friends, co-workers, and colleagues. It is an excellent investment. It pays to pay attention to healthy communication.

Practicing healthy communication skills helps us develop emotional balance that fosters more positive, loving relationships. It also frees up time and energy wasted due to miscommunication, which then can be applied toward uncovering the secrets within us that connect us fully with each other and with our infinite universe. The time and attention you invest in these skills will be greatly appreciated.

Robert Boyer, Ph.D.

SECTION ONE

BASIC PRINCIPLES OF COMMUNICATION

The four chapters in Section I describe a simple framework for the unique *systematic approach to communication* presented in this book. Chapters 1 and 2 briefly introduce the levels of body, mind, heart, and soul and how they relate to each other. Chapter 3 describes the importance of reducing stress in the mind-body system as the platform for applying the skills to foster healthy communication. The final chapter in this section, Chapter 4, deals with how balanced assertiveness promotes smooth and healthy communication, and how imbalanced non-assertiveness and aggressiveness interfere with it. These first four chapters introduce basic principles of the overall approach to communication. The remaining 36 chapters describe specific skills and organize them into the systematic, in-depth approach to use in your everyday life.

The descriptions of basic principles and specific skills include examples of *ineffective* and *effective* uses in real life situations. These examples will help deepen your sense of how to apply the skills in actual communication with other people. The examples will be more helpful if you think through the reasons that a particular example is an *ineffective* or *effective* use of the skill.

Sometimes the reason that a particular example is an ineffective use may not be obvious. This especially could be the case if it is similar to how people you know ordinarily communicate. It also may be similar to how you have learned to communicate by observing people who think they are good communicators. Even many who consider themselves good communicators are not that subtle or refined about how they actually interact with other people. All too often many of them don't listen carefully. Frequently they focus more on giving their own ideas and viewpoints than communicating deeply to enrich relationships. Not being in tune with the deeper levels of behavior, thinking, and feeling results in miscommunication, even among bright and caring people who haven't really learned how to communicate. There are many subtle levels to human interactions, and it takes alert attention and practice to refine the skills so that communication is healthier and more effective.

CHAPTER 1

Feelings, Thoughts, and Behavior

 Feelings, thoughts, and behavior are the building blocks of communication.

1. Communication can be understood simply as the exchange of feelings and thoughts. It is a two-way flow of feelings and thoughts from our inner hearts and minds through outer behavior to other peoples' inner minds and hearts.

2. Impulses rise up from deep within our inner self, soul, or being through the levels of ego, heart, mind and body into behavior. These impulses are first subtle *feelings* that rise up into the heart. In this book, *heart* doesn't mean the circulation pump in the chest, but the inner seat of emotions—the psychological or *feeling* heart. An impulse of feeling rising up in the heart contains a desire or *goal*. It contains the purpose and motivation for action.

3. *Thoughts* are inner impulses rising further from the level of heart to the inner level of mind. Here the word *mind* means the level of thinking and understanding. An impulse of thought in the mind expresses more concretely the feelings coming from deeper in our heart. An impulse of thought in the mind involves a *plan* about how to act to fulfill the heart's goal. In simple terms, feelings express goals—*what to do*—which then become more concrete thoughts that express plans—*how to do it*.

4. *Behavior* refers to outer actions to change the environment according to the mind's plan in order to fulfill the heart's goal. A behavior is an action or movement of the body that can be observed by other people. It refers not only to movement of the whole body such as in walking or running, but also movement of parts of the body such as an arm, eyebrow, or the lips. Behavior is the body's outer action to implement the inner goals and plans at a particular time—*when*—and at a particular place—*where*.

5. Behavior is objective and observable; thoughts and feelings are inner subjective processes that are not observable directly by others. You experience your own feelings and thoughts inside, but other people don't experience directly what you are feeling and thinking. We get clues or signals of what is going on in each others' heart and mind by observing outer behavior, such as attending to body posture and listening to speech.

6. One important type of outer behavior is emotional behavior. Emotions are outer bodily expressions of inner feelings and thoughts. To *emote* means to express inner feelings in outer behavior. When mental impulses are expressed from heart to mind and then into the body, they may produce emotional behavior such as

shouting, laughing, crying, wincing, or smiling. These emotional behaviors may be obvious signs of the underlying feelings and thoughts, or they may not be obvious.

7. Usually several factors need to be considered to identify a particular outer behavior as expressing particular inner feelings and thoughts. Gestures, facial expressions, tone of voice, style of speaking, the meaning of words spoken, and overall circumstances usually all need to be considered. For example, tears may signal sadness or happiness. If they are expressed in a group of friends laughing together, they are likely to be tears of laughter that signal feeling happy and having fun.

8. Some people consider emotions and feelings to be the same thing; this book offers a deeper understanding. Emotions are identified as outer bodily expressions that can be observed by others, and feelings are inner impulses that cannot be observed directly by others. Emotions are observable outer expressions of unobservable inner thoughts and feelings.

9. Healthy communicating involves learning to identify and be clear about your own thoughts and feelings, as well as the thoughts and feelings in other people. This is facilitated by careful attention and listening.

10. Every word we speak and every action we take include all the levels of body, mind, heart, and soul. Speech and other behavior are based on thinking; thinking is based on feeling; feeling is based on being or existence; and individual being is based on universal Being. If we are able to listen fully, every word and action reveal the totality of who we are.

Here is a simple chart that summarizes the basic levels of our individuality.

Levels of the Individual[1]

Outer/Objective	behavior	behaving	when / where
	body		
	senses	sensing	
Inner/Subjective	mind	thinking	how / plan
	heart	feeling	what / goal
	individual self / ego	being	who
		Being	

Examples of How to Use These Principles

EXAMPLE 1

Ineffective use: Ann feels deeply about things, but thinks these feelings are mostly determined by the way people treat her. She thinks that her emotions are sort of automatic reactions, and that she feels what she feels because that's just the way she is. Ann feels controlled by outer circumstances, rather than understanding that her behavior is a product of her inner feelings and thoughts. She frequently feels powerless, and she gets quite annoyed if people don't see how easy it is for her to be hurt by the way other people treat her.

Effective use: Ann realizes that her deep feelings, hopes, and dreams have the power to guide her behavior toward making her life what she wants it to be, rather than being pushed around so much by what other people want. She is starting to recognize that she has inner strengths that help her not be so influenced by small things and by what other people seem to think about her. She is beginning to feel less like a victim of circumstances; she is recognizing that her inner feelings and goals, and inner thoughts and plans, can be more powerful than outer circumstances in the design and direction of her life.

EXAMPLE 2

Ineffective use: Bill and Sheila enjoyed going to theme parks for family vacations when they were kids. Although such trips are now quite expensive, they both see it as an important part of the childhood experience they want their own children to have. They set things up ahead of time to get the best prices and to organize a relatively smooth vacation. But the past two vacations have not been smooth. Even with good planning, their children have seemed distracted and complaining. Bill and Sheila find it frustrating that they are going out of their way to provide a good growing-up experience for the children, but their kids don't seem to appreciate it. They have a set plan about how vacations should be, rather than being flexible about the plan in order to be more successful for their important goal that their children have a positive experience of growing up.

Effective use: Bill and Sheila are beginning to wonder about the cost of the planned family vacation for the upcoming summer, especially if it isn't going to be much fun with their children. They have to commit to the reservations soon. They decide to bring the issue up to the kids. This leads to a spirited discussion about how the kids have felt obligated to do what has been planned because they see how important it is to their parents. In the discussion, the kids bring up their interest in exploring other possibilities for trips together, such as even doing a volunteer project to help others, or exploring new skills in a wilderness experience. Together the family has several discussions about alternatives, brainstorming ideas and giving the positives and negatives.

After two weeks, alternatives are narrowed down and a new plan is developed as a family, which everyone is enthusiastic to try out.

EXAMPLE 3

Ineffective use: Corey is responsible for setting up and conducting the annual meeting to evaluate and establish sales targets for each market region. He works hard to define carefully the goals for each region and a strategy to discuss the best practices for implementing the goals. He hopes to build training support into the budget so that any staff wanting to participate has access to the new best practices.

Effective use: Corey discusses his plans for the meeting with his vice president. The question arises whether something is missing in the approach, even though things have gone okay the last two annual meetings. It is realized that although staff participation in the planning, training, and implementation phases is reasonably good, it might be even more effective to enlist the staff in building the goals for each region. Then the staff may take the goals as their own, and not just goals that they have to accept from management. The human resource trainer is brought into the discussion, and together a new approach is structured that involves more involvement of the staff in setting goals, in addition to establishing plans. It generates a new level of interest and enthusiasm at the annual meeting.

SUMMARY OF CHAPTER 1: Feelings, Thoughts, and Behavior

1. Communication is the exchange of feelings and thoughts.
2. Feelings in the heart relate to goals—what to do.
3. Thoughts in the mind relate to plans—how to do it.
4. Behavior is the outer expression of inner impulses from heart and mind.
5. Behavior is observable, but thoughts and feelings are not.
6. Emotions are the bodily expressions of inner thoughts and feelings.
7. Gestures, postures, voice, and style of speech all signal meaning.
8. To emote means to express inner thoughts and feelings in behavior.
9. Communication requires clarity about your own feelings and thoughts.
10. Every word and every action express all levels of our being.

CHAPTER 2

THE CYCLE OF FEELINGS, THOUGHTS, AND BEHAVIOR

 The cycle of feelings, thoughts, and behavior involves goals, plans, actions, evaluation of results, and degrees of fulfillment.

1. Feelings, thoughts, and behavior work in a cycle. There is an *outward* flow of inner feelings and thoughts that triggers behavior. This outward flow goes from deep within the heart into the mind, and from the mind into the body to express goals and plans. The body then performs actions that produce changes in the environment. The outward flow of impulses of feelings and thoughts expresses into action what can be called mental energy, life force, or life energy coming from deep inside. Life energy naturally flows toward fulfillment of goals and desires for the expansion of happiness. It can be compared to the natural process of a seed blossoming into a flower.

2. Then there is an *inward* flow from the environment back to the mind and heart. Changes in the environment resulting from our behavior are sensed through hearing, touch, sight, taste, and smell. The senses carry information from the outer environment back to the inner mind and heart. In the mind, the information is compared to the original plan and goal. The result of this evaluation is a feeling in the heart according to the degree of success in fulfilling the goal. If the results match the goal, inner feelings of happiness and satisfaction result, and we tend to feel better about our selves.

3. Thus we have a desire for something, we think about how to get it, and then we act. The results of the action are compared to the original goal and plan, and we experience some degree of fulfillment. If the results don't match the goal, we may try out a new action, plan, or goal. The experience of some level of fulfillment motivates another cycle to gain even higher levels of fulfillment.

4. In this simple model, both heart and mind have two roles. The heart produces the goal that motivates behavior, and enjoys the experience of fulfillment. The mind produces the plan to fulfill the heart's goal, and evaluates the results of behavior.

5. The heart is concerned primarily with the sense of love, appreciation, and creating happiness. It *enfolds*, accepts, and unifies. It is also involved in intuitive aspects of decision making.

6. The mind is concerned primarily with the sense of duty, responsibility, and getting things done correctly. It *unfolds*, understands, and specifies. It has the primary task of decision making and problem solving in order to coordinate the goals of the heart with the requirements of the environment. Importantly, the heart guides the mind, but the mind directs behavior.

7. The outward and inward cycle of feelings, thoughts, and behavior repeats itself again and again with bigger goals, better plans, and more effective actions toward higher levels of fulfillment. Usually there are several goals and plans at the same time as we work toward permanent fulfillment in our life.
8. For example, let's say you want to talk with your friend. You call her home, learn she is working at the store, drive there, and chat during her break. The goal was to talk with your friend; the plan was to find out how to do it. When your behavior satisfied the plan and goal, your feelings were expressed in emotional behavior of smiling and a warm hello to your friend.
9. For another example, let's say you want to build a youth center to help your community. You plan an outdoor concert fundraiser, but it rains and has to be canceled. So you try a new plan, this time a big radio auction of donated goods and services. With a large donation, the funds are raised and the youth center is built. You feel fulfilled by accomplishing your goal of helping your community.
10. Your heart's goal was to improve the community by building a youth center. Your mind's plan was first a concert and then an auction. Your behavior included setting up the concert, canceling it, running the auction, and collecting donations. The results were compared to the goal and they matched. Feelings of fulfillment are naturally expressed in emotional behavior, such as thanking helpers and donors.

Adding this cycle to the chart from Chapter 1:

Outward and Inward Cycle of Communication

	Levels of the Individual		Inward/Outward Cycle	
Outer/ Objective	behavior	behaving	action	results of action
	body		↑	↓
	·······senses·······	·······sensing·······		
Inner/ Subjective	mind	thinking	plan	evaluation
	heart	feeling	goal	fulfillment
	individual self / ego	being	I (have)	sense of self
			↑	↓
	Being			

Examples of How to Use These Principles

EXAMPLE 1

Ineffective use: Jim recognizes that his life is his own, to make of it what he wants. But he doesn't really know what he wants. He is not clear about what is important, and isn't in tune with what is deeply fulfilling and worthwhile in his life. He thinks that he might as well just wait and see what happens and, in the meantime, have as much fun as he can by partying a lot. He doesn't feel very good about his life, which he sees as directionless and kind of stagnant, but at least he can hang out with friends and have a little fun.

Effective use: Jim realizes that his buddies also want more happiness, just like he does. But they also don't know how to create it. He has noticed, however, that a couple of his friends seem to have clearer goals. Somehow their lives are a little more focused and together, and they seem to be a little happier too. Jim decides to go up to the lake in the mountains for some quiet time to reflect deeply about what he wants to accomplish for himself and the world.

EXAMPLE 2

Ineffective use: Ralph and Judy are so busy during the week that they don't have time to organize for family weekends. They like the spontaneity of not having everything structured. Their children see them only a little during the week, however, and expect that on weekends their parents will set things up for the family to do. But when nothing gets organized, the kids end up hanging out with friends. Ralph and Judy assume the kids are busy, and end up resting some and occasionally doing cleaning projects. Not much happens with the family together, and home life begins to be boring, fragmented, and at times more tense.

Effective use: Ralph and Judy let their children know that they want to spend at least some time with them most every weekend. Together the family thinks of some ideas about what might be fun, and a quick plan is set up for the next month to try out. It turns out that on two of the weekends the weather doesn't cooperate, but the other two weekends do result in family activities that everyone agrees were kind of fun. They agree to try again for two weekends next month, this time with weather contingency plans.

EXAMPLE 3

Ineffective use: Steve is very clear about how important it is for him to do the best he possibly can with grades in his junior college classes. He knows that his chances of getting into law school depend on them. He has carefully chosen the sequence of courses, and is even using the time between semesters to get a head start on the next courses he will take. He has been feeling a bit tired of it all, however, and at times has been daydreaming more while studying. He even imagines going to some remote island to live, possibly as a fisherman—although he has never had any interest in fishing in his life.

Effective use: Steve decides he will contact a couple of the law professors at the university to find out their professional and personal interests, and how they maintain enthusiasm for their work. One of them puts him in touch with a law firm that sometimes helps well-motivated students work with its law firm partners in volunteer projects for the community. Steve begins to learn how to focus on activities that are fun and interesting for him and that also support his interest in legal training. He is learning to coordinate better his goals, plans, and actions.

SUMMARY OF CHAPTER 2: The Cycle of Feelings, Thoughts, and Behavior

1. Life energy flows outward from heart and mind into behavior.
2. There is an inward flow from the environment back to mind and heart.
3. We have a desire, plan how to fulfill it, and take action.
4. This cycle involves goals, plans, evaluation, and fulfillment.
5. The heart is primarily concerned with the sense of love.
6. The mind is primarily concerned with the sense of duty.
7. This cycle repeats itself toward higher degrees of fulfillment.
8. Feelings are naturally expressed in emotional behavior.
9. The mind builds the plan and evaluates the results.
10. The heart develops the goal and enjoys its fulfillment.

CHAPTER 3
INCREASING THE POSITIVE INFLUENCE OF FEELINGS, THOUGHTS, AND BEHAVIOR

 Increasing the positive influence of feelings, thoughts, and behavior refers to working with body, mind, and heart in sequence to open up deeper communication.

1. To fulfill plans and goals effectively, heart, mind, and body need to work well with each other. When the heart's goal, the mind's plan, and the body's actions are not well coordinated, it is harder to achieve goals and increase happiness. This inevitably occurs when stress interferes with feelings, thoughts, and behavior. Stress refers to the damaging influence of strain and tension from trying to cope with challenging circumstances.

2. Stress can be compared to *noise* in the transmission and reception of radio or television signals. Signals get distorted or noisy when the machinery for sending and receiving information doesn't work properly. In the human mind-body system, stress weakens feelings, thoughts, and behavior.

3. In engineering theories of communication, an important principle is the *signal-to noise* ratio. According to this principle, communication is improved both by reducing noise and by producing a stronger signal. Lower noise and higher signal strength result in better communication. In us, reduced noise means less stress. And higher signal strength can be associated with applying skills that produce more powerful communication signals.

4. A settled, low-stressed body, mind, and heart is the best platform for communication signals to be received and sent. Useful methods to reduce stress include adequate sleep, healthy diet, regular exercise, avoidance of addictions, and regular daily routines. Scientifically validated stress reduction techniques also can significantly increase inner silence and reduce mental and physical *noise*.

5. With rested bodies and more inner silence, it becomes easier to apply communication skills to increase positive communication signals. Highly stressed people don't have the clarity of mind or patience of heart to use communication skills when needed. Sometimes they even forget how fulfilling it is to communicate openly from heart to heart. It is a real loss in life when communication is no longer easy due to noisy hearts and minds.

6. Most of the skills in this book focus on increasing the strength of communication signals, and a few of them focus on reducing noise. By applying these skills, you will send stronger and clearer signals so it is easier for people to understand you. This also will help others understand themselves better, which helps them send stronger, clearer signals back to you.

7. The systematic approach to communication is to work in a sequence with other people, first dealing with outer levels and then inner levels. First attend to the outer level of body and behavior, especially emotional behavior, then the level of mind and thinking, and then the deeper level of heart and feeling. Once things are more settled and there is a good mutual connection on the level of heart and feeling, then work in the outward direction of heart, mind, and behavior with mutual goals and plans in cooperative behavior.

8. Deeper communication results when emotions are settled. It is very important to understand that if you try to problem solve with another person when either of you have strong unsettled emotions, it can quickly deteriorate into miscommunication. Like central processors in computers, the human information processing system processes one thing at a time—either output or input. With strong emotions, energy is moving outward. Information is being sent rather than received, and this makes it difficult to receive information. When energy is being outputted such as through speech, it is as if the ears are not connected to the central processor (mind) to receive input. People don't listen well when they are unsettled and have strong emotions.

9. Once things settle down and there is a deeper exchange of thoughts and feelings, then emotional expressions become smoother. Speech style, voice, facial expressions, and gestures become more open, reflecting more trust, appreciation, and respect. The mind opens up when it is cool and calm. When the body and emotions are settled and the mind is cool and calm, then naturally the heart engages in deeper, more fulfilling communication. The heart opens up when it is warm and safe. Healthy communication involves a *warm heart* and a *cool mind*.[2] Opening up these deeper levels takes time, but the benefits are well worth it.

10. This book is organized to train communication skills in the sequence from outer to inner levels, first on the level of body and behavior, then mind, then heart. Later in the book, the focus will be on the outward direction of expressing mutual goals, plans, and behavior from heart to mind to action. At the end of the book are the deepest skills, related to the level of soul and being. These skills naturally develop inner balance and refinement that foster smoother and healthier communication, and they help us progress more rapidly toward permanent fulfillment.

Examples of How to Use These Principles

EXAMPLE 1

Ineffective use: Sonya feels that she and her husband get along reasonably well, but don't really communicate deeply about important topics, at least in the way some people on afternoon TV talk shows try to describe. She wants to be able to have much more open talks with him on a regular basis. She decides to get him to agree to sit down and talk with her at least 20 minutes after he gets home from work on Mondays, Wednesdays, and Fridays. On the first Monday evening, she proposes the plan to her husband and asks him to talk about whether he is happy with the people he works with at the office. Her husband tries, but quickly gets frustrated and an argument ensues, at which point Sonya walks out and calls her sister to complain about it.

Effective use: Sonya tells her husband one evening that she would like to show more support for his work and his creative ideas for improving the business. Her husband expresses appreciation for her interest. She asks how and when to talk about it, and he says perhaps the first thing would be to ask if he wants to talk about work at that time. Most evenings he says he is tired and doesn't want to talk about his work. But over the next month, they do have two conversations that she and her husband feel went pretty well.

EXAMPLE 2

Ineffective use: Eddie doesn't like arguing with his dad, so he tries to keep things cool by hanging out downtown and coming home after his dad turns off the TV and goes to bed, which is usually quite late. His parents work hard and need to get rest, so Eddie tries not to bug them. But then he gets yelled at for not doing anything around the house. He does his best to stay out of his parents' way and can't understand why they criticize him, rather than just returning the favor and staying out of his way.

Effective use: Eddie begins to question his approach when he notices things are less tense at his friend Wally's house. Wally is fun to spend time with, and he also seems to have a little more energy. He doesn't stay out late because he gets up early to take care of his animals. Wally said he worked out a deal with his dad to have dinner with his mom and sisters when his dad is out of town for work. In return, his dad does something fun with him each weekend. Wally says it works out pretty well, and that he and his dad are getting along better. When Eddie decides to bring up to his dad the idea of doing some things together, his dad seems happy about it, which surprises and encourages Eddie.

EXAMPLE 3

Ineffective use: Irene realizes she needs to develop better communication skills to be successful at her new job, which is much more social than the data input position she had for the past five years. She joins the local church group that meets twice a week to study together, and she also joins a public speaking club that meets weekly. With these additional activities she is now quite a bit busier in the evenings, but feels she is progressing on her goals more quickly. However, two of her co-workers have mentioned this week that she seems a bit more tired and irritable than she did in the first few months of the new job.

Effective use: Irene recognizes that her new evening schedule is using too much energy in her efforts to develop better social skills. She decides to cut back to two evenings per week, and to rest a little more the other evenings. She also starts meeting regularly with human resource staff at work to talk about the skills she needs to develop. She finds that this is helping her connect with several other staff people, and is increasing her comfort and confidence at work. She has gone to lunch with two new people over the past month, a major step. She is recognizing how to bring more balance to her life with proper rest and activity, which is supporting her progress on developing better social skills.

SUMMARY OF CHAPTER 3: Increasing the Positive Influence of Feelings, Thoughts, and Behavior

1. Stress clouds and distorts feelings, thoughts, and behavior.
2. Low noise and high signal strength result in better communication.
3. Low stress in the mind-body system fosters healthy communication.
4. Inner silence and rest reduces stress or noise in heart, mind, and body.
5. The skills in this book increase the strength of communication signals
6. Work with the levels of behavior, mind, and heart in sequence.
7. Deeper communication results from a more settled mind-body system.
8. With deep communication, strong positive emotions can be expressed.
9. This book is structured in the sequence of outer to inner levels.
10. Healthy communication involves using this sequence systematically.

CHAPTER 4
THE FLOW OF FEELINGS, THOUGHTS, AND BEHAVIOR

 The flow of feelings, thoughts, and behavior refers to how life energy is expressed through the levels of heart, mind, and body.

1. In the natural cycle of the flow of life energy, inner feelings and thoughts are expressed outwardly, from deep within the heart into the mind and then into behavior. Deeper levels are subtler and more powerful—like going from molecular power to atomic power. Deeper communication requires a smooth, balanced flow of mental energy or life energy.

2. When there is a smooth flow of energy through heart, mind, body, and behavior, goals and plans are more effectively expressed. This is called a balanced or assertive style of behavior. In this style, these levels work together in well-planned action, and they result in healthier relationships.

3. Assertiveness is associated with actualizing or expressing one's inner potential. It involves clarity about one's own goals, proper planning, and implementing goals in behavior that coordinates well with the goals of others. Assertiveness refers to emotional balance of the outward and inward flow of life energy.

4. Sometimes due to stress an unhealthy pattern of holding in energy develops. This imbalanced pattern is called non-assertive behavior. In this style, people are hesitant to act on their own goals. They tend to internalize blame, and are overly concerned about making embarrassing mistakes or going against the goals of others. They find it difficult to stand up for themselves at the times when it is important to do so. They withdraw or hold back on their own goals in a mistaken attempt to help others, rather than cooperating on mutual goals.

5. Because it is natural to express life energy and unnatural to hold it back, pressure builds up in the form of frustration and resentment. Energy is spent holding things in, or stuffing emotions, which results in feeling held down or even depressed. Less energy gets through heart into mind and behavior, so it is harder to plan, decide and act to fulfill one's own goals. Over time, the cycle of feelings, thoughts, and behavior toward more fulfillment can bog down, and healthy daily routines get disrupted. Anxiety and even panic can develop about not being able to hold it all inside. In the extreme, this non-assertive pattern can lead to social isolation—as if imprisoned in self-imposed restrictions, even fearing such activities as going to the market or visiting family and friends.

6. On the other hand, sometimes due to stress an unhealthy pattern of expressing goals without adequate planning in the mind develops. This imbalanced style is called aggressive behavior. In this style, people don't think things through before acting. Behavior is impulsive and rough, such as destructive anger. Because behav-

ior is not well-planned, it doesn't fit smoothly into the environment and has damaging effects on relationships.

7. Aggressive people tend to be quite oversensitive or touchy on a deep level of feeling. For example, the bully on the block is frequently the most over-sensitive, putting up a harsh, defensive façade to hide it. Aggressive people can attack or manipulate others to avoid dealing with their own self-doubts, showing little patience or respect for the plans and goals of others. They tend to externalize blame, and try to control others by ignoring them or using them for their own selfish goals. Aggressive behavior can be abusive. When the rights of others are violated, aggressive people can become subject to restrictions imposed by the laws of society. In the extreme, sometimes they are removed from society and imprisoned for a while, in the hope they can learn to manage behavior in a more assertively balanced way that doesn't harm others.

8. Usually behavior is not just one of these styles, but shifts between them. Frequently there is a mixture of assertive and non-assertive behavior for a while, during which frustration and resentment slowly build up inside. At some point they burst out in aggressiveness, then return to non-assertiveness. It is under-reacting and over-reacting, rather than balanced assertiveness. Also, sometimes aggressiveness is indirect, such as not being straightforward or honest, called a passive-aggressive style. These styles show up in individual interactions between people, and sometimes long-term personality patterns. They also occur between groups of people, and even between nations.

9. It is easier to be assertive on the level of thinking than on the deeper, more delicate but powerful level of feeling. But balanced assertiveness on the level of feeling in the heart is very important for healthy relationships. People who non-assertively withdraw tend to draw out aggression in others. On the other hand, pushy aggressive people contribute to non-assertiveness in others—for a while. Such imbalances create anger, resentment, mental and physical stress, break-ups in business and personal relationships, and sometimes abusive behavior.

10. With deeper inner silence through reduced stress, balanced assertiveness is easier. The ability to use communication skills in a timely manner grows. A smooth, balanced, naturally assertive flow of energy through heart, mind, and body fosters success in one's own goals while also helping others achieve their goals in healthy mutual cooperation. Decreasing inner noise and increasing communication signals result in deeper, healthier, and more fulfilling relationships.

Examples of How to Use These Principles

EXAMPLE 1

Ineffective use: Reid is in his second year of marriage, loves his new wife, and wants things to go well. However, he is finding that having to take into consideration her moods and her wishes is a bit complicating. In his single life he did what he wanted, when he wanted, without having to worry much about what others feel or think. Now he sometimes feels like everything is about her. He decides that he needs to get back to doing what he wants to do, and his wife needs to learn how to fit into his life. He comes to the conclusion that he needs to start handling things more directly, like he used to do. But rather than assertive balance, he becomes aggressive. Confused by this, his wife begins to feel more distant from him. Reid reacts with more suspicion about her, wondering if she really loves him.

Effective use: Reid realizes that he has never really learned how to be in a close relationship of any kind. All his life he has just pretty much done what he wanted to do, and people accepted or rejected it as they wish, without him caring a heck of a lot either way. Now he does care a lot about his wife, and her reactions are important to him. It's a new level of commitment than he has had before, and it requires a more balanced and mature approach to communication. He decides to work on his relationship skills, including learning how and when to express his own wants to his wife. He decides his first step is to read one or two relationship communication books to find out if there is anything practical in them.

EXAMPLE 2

Ineffective use: Marina is recognizing that her children run over her all the time, and it is getting out of hand. She is tired, and is feeling a little down lately. She works so hard to help her children, caring for them in every way possible as a good mother. But they show little appreciation, and even little interest at all in home life, just wanting to be with friends. Marina decides it is time to crack down and show them who is boss again. She begins to set up a list of house rules including not talking to her disrespectfully, which her children completely ignore, making the tension at home even higher.

Effective use: As things get even more tense in the home after trying to impose the new rules, Marina sees that her strategy of trying to be more assertive with her children is not working. The kids complain that she has been too bossy and controlling all of a sudden, and they are even more disrespectful toward her. She decides that a more effective strategy of balanced assertiveness is to contact a parenting communication specialist and develop better skills to apply with herself and her children. She realizes she needs training to learn the skills of how to assert herself better as a parent.

EXAMPLE 3

Ineffective use: Ralph was promoted to supervisor because of his excellent work record as a machinist. He gets things done; and in this spirit he takes seriously the new responsibility he has been given from management. But he becomes quite frustrated when employees don't automatically share his standards, and he needs to push them to strive for quality in their work. Ralph is also finding it harder to meet production levels because absenteeism and turnover are rising. Also, on a personal level, he has noticed some difficulty sleeping, as well as more bickering with his teenage son.

Effective use: While on a fishing trip, Ralph and his brother talk about becoming a better manager by managing oneself first. Ralph begins to wonder if he is in fact creating inefficiency by the more tense, aggressive, and critical style that has crept into his work as a supervisor. He decides that a good place to start is to make a point of turning off the TV and going to bed earlier, in order to be more rested and to take better care of himself. He realizes this may help him be more balanced at work, be a more effective supervisor, and also he may have a little more energy and patience to deal with the increasingly challenging behavior of his son.

SUMMARY OF CHAPTER 4: The Flow of Feelings, Thoughts, and Behavior

1. Deeper levels of mind and heart are more powerful.
2. Assertive balance is the smooth flow of energy or life force.
3. Non-assertiveness is holding back energy.
4. Aggressiveness is acting without proper planning.
5. Many people shift between non-assertive and aggressive behavior.
6. Assertiveness is easier on the level of mind than the level of heart.
7. Assertiveness supports fulfillment of goals in oneself and in others.
8. Many people shift from one of the patterns to another through time.
9. Non-assertiveness draws out aggressiveness in others, and vice versa.
10. Assertive balance develops with less stress and more inner silence.

Putting It All Together

Basic Principles of Communication

Energy flows through us from inner to outer, from deep within the feeling level of the heart to the thinking level of the mind, to be expressed in outer observable behavior. This is the expressive or outward flow of communication, associated with sending information.

This sequence of the outer flow of communication involves goals of what we want to do, plans of how to accomplish the goals, and actions in the environment to fulfill the plans and goals. When this outward flow is smooth, we are able to express our own goals and plans with balanced assertiveness. We are able to cooperate effectively with others as they also express their own goals and plans.

The inward flow of energy from outer to inner is associated with receiving information. In terms of the systematic approach to communication in this book, this involves attending to the outer level of body and behaving, especially body language and emotional behavior, then the level of thinking in the mind associated with solution building, and then the deeper inner level of feeling in the heart related to positive feelings of love and devotion.

Healthy, effective communication is fostered through reducing inner noise in the mind-body system and increasing the strength of communication signals. We then become better listeners in receiving information, and also better senders of information. The natural result of a balanced, assertive flow of energy through heart, mind, and body is communication that is more open, smooth, effective, and mutually fulfilling. Healthy communication naturally results from a warm heart and a cool mind.

Some people can develop a non-assertive communication style of not standing up for themselves, and living for others without being happy about it. Others can develop an aggressive style of not considering others' feelings, and basically treating others disrespectfully. Both of these imbalanced styles result in miscommunication, conflict, stress, and unhappiness.

Communication skills are simple tools that help make the flow of energy smoother, within and between people. When there is a smooth flow of energy in balanced assertiveness, communication is healthier and more effective. Then there is less need to use communication skills in a formal way, because their purpose is already being accomplished. When this is not occurring, the skills help create balance in communication. However, even very skilled communicators can benefit from applying basic communication skills to maintain assertive balance. On occasion, it is quite helpful to go back to the most basic communication skills, in the same way that a professional athlete sometimes needs to reestablish the basics in order to maintain excellence in performance.

The points in the past four chapters on basic principles of communication are summarized in the chart below. In this chart, there is an added column that lists the categories of skills to be covered in the rest of the book. The chart shows the relationship between the levels of communication and the categories of skills that generally relate to each of the levels. Also added is an underlying level of universal Self associated with Being, to be discussed briefly at the end of the book.

A main theme of this systematic approach to communication is to apply the skills in a sequence from outer to inner levels in receiving information from others, and then inner to outer levels in sending information and working with others to share goals and plans in effective teamwork. This results in deeper, healthier communication and in balanced, mutually fulfilling relationships.

Levels of the Individual and Corresponding Communication Skills

Levels of the Individual			Inward/Outward Cycle		Communication Skills
Outer/ Objective	behavior	behaving	action	results of action	Attending Skills
					Engaging Skills
	body		↑	↓	Listening Skills
					Emotion Management Skills
	senses	sensing			
Inner/ Subjective	mind	thinking	plan	evaluation	Solution Skills
	heart	feeling	goal	fulfillment	Empowering Skills
	individual self/ ego	being	I (have) ↑	sense of self ↓	Actualizing Skills
	universal Self	Being			

SECTION TWO

COMMUNICATION SKILLS ON THE LEVEL OF BODY AND BEHAVING

This second section of the book begins the training in how to apply the basic principles of healthy communication in the 36 specific skills, starting with the outer level of communication. This level relates to observable behavior in the body that expresses unobservable inner thoughts and feelings in the mind and heart. It includes attending, engaging, listening, and emotion management skills. The sequence of chapters and the skills follow the sequence of unfolding deeper levels of communication.

The skills in this section can be understood to be more introductory or preliminary. They will help you observe and listen more attentively; they provide useful information for the deeper skills in the next section. However, very good observers of body signals can get information about people's thoughts in a way that they even seem to read other peoples' minds.

When approaching a person, the outermost levels such as body posture, gestures, and facial expressions are typically observed first. Next usually the tone of voice and content of speech can be heard. As you engage in talking, the emotional behavior of the person is more noticeable. You can communicate more deeply by effectively dealing with emotions.

The first skills in this section, called attending skills, involve observing outer non-verbal and verbal behaviors as indicators or signals of inner thoughts and feelings. The category of attending skills includes attending to gestures, attending to facial expressions, attending to voice, and attending to speech. The second set of skills in this section, called engaging skills, involves simple approaches that foster communication. This includes the skills of listening, prompting, questioning, and matching. Attending and engaging skills will help you attend more carefully to the process of communicating and become a better observer.

The skills that follow after the attending and engaging skills are key skills to focus on and learn well. Those next skills, called listening and emotion management skills, are very important skills to develop and use regularly for healthy, effective communication. Listening skills that promote deeper communication include summarizing, validating, and empathizing. Emotion management skills that help settle down and manage emotions include disarming, disengaging, venting, grounding, and resetting. Listening and emotion management skills are core basic skills of the systematic approach to communication in this book.

ATTENDING SKILLS

Attending skills involve observing non-verbal behaviors such as gestures or body postures and facial expressions, as well as verbal behaviors such as voice tone and speech style. These are the initial skills to apply as you first approach people to begin communicating with them. The skills provide helpful clues for understanding other peoples' inner thoughts and feelings. Included are skills associated with observing gestures, facial expressions, voice, and style of speech.

CHAPTER 5
ATTENDING TO GESTURES

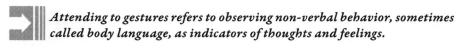*Attending to gestures refers to observing non-verbal behavior, sometimes called body language, as indicators of thoughts and feelings.*

1. People don't always put into words what they are feeling and thinking. This is sometimes due to not being clear about their own thoughts and feelings, not knowing how to put them into words, or not wanting to reveal them. However, there are many indicators of feelings and thoughts in addition to speech or verbal communication.

2. Important outer clues about inner feelings and thoughts are frequently reflected in non-verbal behaviors such as gestures and body postures. People don't usually like to be stared at, but simply noticing gestures can help in communicating with other people.

3. In general, relaxed and open gestures correspond to openness in mind and heart. Assertive balance is reflected in relaxed, comfortable gestures. Arms open and away from the body or loose to the side, legs comfortably crossed while sitting, hands easily folded together, fingers steepled together, and hand gestures displaying the palms all suggest openness to communicate and to exchange thoughts and feelings.

4. Comfortably leaning toward another person suggests being interested in or moving toward the person emotionally. Sitting toward the front of the chair facing another person, with the head slightly tilted or resting on the hands, suggests attentive openness. Eye contact without much tightness and tension around the eyes also suggests openness and interest.

5. Non-assertiveness is reflected in more restricted and closed or protective gestures, suggesting restricted thoughts and feelings. When the body is rigid, such as arms firmly crossed on the chest or legs wrapped around the chair, it suggests anxious, closed feelings and thoughts. Restriction of body movement is an indicator of trying to hide feelings. Hands and arms are used less to illustrate what is being said. However, an overly relaxed, limp posture of slumping down also can be an indicator of a non-assertive, down feeling.

6. Leaning or moving away from another person suggests moving away emotionally; leaning toward the door suggests wanting to leave. Leaning heavily on objects such as a chair or wall suggests feeling off balance or needing support. Looking away, or sliding feet back and forth, suggests wanting to walk away. A sudden very pale facial tone sometimes indicates non-assertive uneasiness, anxiety, or fear. Non-assertive uneasiness and trying to hide feelings are also suggested by all the following gestures: avoiding eye contact, fidgeting, leg shaking or kicking, lip biting, shoul-

der shrugging, hair twisting, nose or ear rubbing, playing with objects such as a pen or eye glasses, putting fingers in or near the mouth, throat clearing, frequent blinking, rapid and irregular breathing, perspiring, or swallowing.

7. Aggressiveness is reflected in quick, intense gestures, indicating defensiveness or offensive attack. Stiffening up, standing taller and rigid, quick moves, hard stares, or pointing fingers suggest aggressiveness. Angry, argumentative people use the finger like a sword. Sudden redness of skin tone is sometimes associated with anger, but sometimes embarrassment. If someone appears from these cues to be angry, stand toward the person's side to give the feeling of being on his or her side. Standing over others suggests trying to have aggressive authority or control over them. It is natural for small children to look up to adults, but it interferes with communicating on an equal basis. Sit down at about equal height to talk on the same level.

8. If someone puts his face close to yours, or touches you such that you feel uncomfortable, it suggests trying to manipulate in an aggressive way. Standing at least an arm's length is usually a comfortable social distance. Being closer is appropriate for personal friends and intimate partners—when both feel comfortable—but otherwise can contribute to feeling invaded. If you have to be close due to lack of space, ask or excuse yourself. Touching such as in handshaking or hugging typically lasts a few seconds, and suggests trying to control the person if it persists much longer. Until you know that physical contact is comfortable to the other person, positive words and smiles are more respectful.

9. There are three general questions regarding gestures and postures:
    A.   Open or closed?
    B.   Relaxed or rigid?
    C.   Toward you or away?

10. Relationships between non-verbal behaviors and inner feelings and thoughts vary with individual and cultural differences. In some cultures, looking directly in the eyes of an elder is considered disrespectful. In others, looking away is disrespectful. If you don't know the local customs, people usually appreciate being asked. As you spend time observing others, you can learn what the specific gestures and postures signal about their inner thoughts and feelings.

Examples of How to Use This Skill

EXAMPLE 1

Ineffective use: Diane assumed that Sheila probably didn't like her and didn't want to sit near her. Diane came to this conclusion when she saw Sheila cross her arms and look away toward the door as soon as Diane walked into the room and toward Sheila to sit down next to her.

Effective use: As Diane headed toward the empty seat next to Sheila, she noticed that Sheila seemed to tighten up and look away. Diane asked if the seat was available. Sheila replied yes, but quickly asked sheepishly if Diane saw Michael outside in the hall, because she was hoping Michael might sit next to her today. She whispered to Diane that she just heard Michael might be interested in her, and that she'd tell Diane about it later that afternoon. Diane then understood the reason Sheila seemed to tighten up as she walked toward her and didn't want her to take the next seat. She now felt comfortable about not sitting next to Sheila, and was eager to talk with her later about the news about Michael.

EXAMPLE 2

Ineffective use: As Georgette sees her husband walking up to the front door after getting off work, she notes that he is almost stomping up the porch steps. As he enters the house, she remarks, 'Well, it looks like you are all tense and angry again. It must've been another tough day; I suppose you'll expect supper right away.'

Effective use: Seeing her husband come into the house moving quickly and rigidly, Georgette thinks that he may very likely be tense. She has learned that at these times her assertive response is to express briefly a little openness and warmth, but then leave him alone for a few minutes so he can settle himself down. She states, 'Hi, honey. Would you like some tea? I'll be out on the back porch for a while.'

EXAMPLE 3

Ineffective use: When John comes into Denise's office to talk about his vacation schedule, Denise notices that he seems to be distracted and not paying attention. He is looking around the room, and hardly even looking at her. She thinks John may be showing disrespect for her. She comments: 'I've got a lot to do today, John, what is it you want to talk about now?'

Effective use: When John comes into Denise's office and sits to talk about his vacation schedule, Denise notices that John is fidgeting with his pen a lot, and is glancing around the room without looking directly at her. She senses he may be uncomfortable about the meeting. She makes a comment about something that went well in his department last month. After seeing John relax back into the chair a bit, she comments that he has a week and a half of vacation time left this year, and since August is their busiest month, she wants to sort out with him the best time to fit in his remaining vacation days. As John feels more comfortable, supported by Denise's communication skill, he is able to work smoothly with her on the vacation schedule.

SUMMARY OF CHAPTER 5: Attending to Gestures

1. People don't always express feelings and thoughts in their speech.
2. Non-verbal gestures are important clues to feelings and thoughts.
3. Relaxed, open gestures suggest assertive openness in mind and heart.
4. Leaning toward physically suggests leaning toward emotionally.
5. Restricted gestures suggest non-assertiveness and closed mindedness.
6. Leaning away physically suggests leaning away emotionally.
7. Tense, stiff, and rapid gestures suggest aggressiveness.
8. Being too close and touching physically suggests aggressive control.
9. Basic issues on gestures: open/closed; relaxed/rigid; toward/away.
10. Learn cultural customs before trying to interpret gestures.

CHAPTER 6
ATTENDING TO FACIAL EXPRESSIONS

 Attending to facial expressions refers to observing patterns of relaxed and tense muscles in the face as indicators of inner thoughts and feelings.

1. After attending to gestures and postures, the next type of behavior to attend to is facial expressions. People young and old all over the world have very similar facial expressions that generally reflect similar thoughts and feelings. Attending to facial expressions can provide helpful information about peoples' emotions and deeper inner feelings. Some experts think facial expressions, body language, and voice style provide even more reliable information than words about inner thoughts and feelings.

2. In general, an upward pull of facial muscles is suggestive of positive, assertive thoughts and feelings. A downward pull is suggestive of negative thoughts and feelings, usually associated with non-assertiveness or aggressiveness.

3. Over time, frequently experienced emotions can actually get sort of sculpted into the face. You may notice in some people a permanent expression suggestive of happiness, sadness, worry, or frustration. Sometimes even one side of the face subtly suggests one emotion and the other side another emotion, such as anger and sadness or interest and suspicion. Similarly, a protruding jaw is sometimes suggestive of an aggressive pattern and a receding jaw is suggestive of non-assertiveness.

4. The eyes have been described as the windows to the soul because many times they reflect thoughts and feelings more clearly than other aspects of gestures and postures. Muscles around the eyes frequently give better signals about thoughts and feelings than muscles around the mouth. Generally an upward pull of muscles around the eyes suggests positive, assertive thoughts and feelings, whereas a downward pull suggests the opposite.

5. The pupils in the eyes become larger when something of interest is seen, such as when someone attractive is seen or a mother sees a baby. Length of eye contact suggests degree of interest. Prolonged eye contact suggests more intense interactions between people, such as lovers gazing deeply into each other's eyes. However, intense stares with squinting eyes and tight neck and shoulder muscles suggest defensiveness and aggression—it is a warning signal of attack in the animal world. Displaying teeth, other than smiling, is also sometimes suggestive of warning or threat.

6. Smiling typically suggests assertive appreciation and acceptance, and also tends to increase attractiveness. However, it is useful to distinguish between genuine and social smiles. In a genuine smile, the entire face pulls upward. And in a social smile,

cheek muscles pull upward but eye muscles typically don't. Social smiles appear polite, but may hide negative thoughts and feelings such as suspicion, anger, or jealousy.

7. An opened mouth while listening suggests that there may be some difficulty taking in the information. Either there is too much information, or it is hard to swallow. Biting the lips frequently suggests holding back emotions in a non-assertive manner. Running the tongue over the lips may be a signal of wanting to take in something, such as wanting to give some idea additional consideration and thought.

8. The neck is a very vulnerable part of the body. When the neck is exposed, it frequently suggests assertive thoughts and feelings of trust and safety. When people feel safe in a conversation, their heads are often bent slightly, exposing the side of the neck. When something disagreeable or threatening is said, frequently the head is quickly moved to protect the neck. When shoulders are pulled up and the chin is down—like a boxer—it suggests aggressive defensiveness. But when the nose is pointed up into the air with exposed neck, it may suggest defiance and trying to portray fearlessness.

9. Sighing is a complex expression that can be suggestive of trying to accept something that is challenging. When people sigh, sometimes they are trying to accept what is being said at the moment, or acknowledging some other challenging issue in their lives, whether it is negative or positive.

10. In interpreting facial expressions, perhaps the most basic issue is whether there is an upward pull of muscles in the face, generally associated with positive emotions and balanced assertiveness, or a downward pull of muscles, more indicative of negative emotions and non-assertiveness. Permanent facial features may also provide helpful clues to long-term individual personality patterns. When attending to facial expressions, it is helpful also to consider gestures, voice, speech, and the overall situation in interpreting what they signal about inner thoughts and feelings.

Examples of How to Use This Skill

EXAMPLE 1

Ineffective use: Mona was very impressed to be working in the office of a prominent leader such as Bill. He made a point of glancing at her and smiling discretely when he came through the office. Mona knew she shouldn't stare back at him. But on the other hand, she did feel very special to get attention from this powerful and charismatic man.

Effective use: The next week when Bill returned to the office, Mona noticed that he gave a more direct and intense look at her. For the first time, he also said hello and actually called her by name. Mona was a little taken aback by this apparent change in Bill's level of interest toward her. In talking with other staff about what was going on with Bill, she happened to find out that he and his wife might be having marital problems. Mona decided to be a little more alert and cautious when interacting with him.

EXAMPLE 2

Ineffective use: Angela thought that her daughter, Tina, was comfortable with her instructions to pick her clothes up from the floor, because Tina had leaned her head to one side and exposed her neck, postures that can be indicative of openness and receptivity.

Effective use: When Angela's daughter leaned her head to the side and exposed her neck in response to Angela's instructions to pick up her clothes, Angela also noticed her daughter then crossed her arms and stiffened up. Angela then thought that the head-leaning gesture might be signaling defiance in the context of the other body signals. She then asked her daughter if there was something immediate that her daughter needed to take care of first.

EXAMPLE 3

Ineffective use: Smitty had developed somewhat of a pattern of getting back to his work station a few minutes late after lunch. He assumed it was no big deal, because whenever his supervisor saw him returning a little late there still seemed to be a polite smile on him.

Effective use: Smitty noticed when he got back early from lunch one day that his supervisor seemed actually to have a little bit more genuine and full smile on his face. He also openly interacted with Smitty for a moment, which was somewhat unusual. Smitty decided it might be worth stopping in to discuss with his supervisor how precise he was expected to be about the lunch hour. He wanted to be sure that no negative impressions were building up in the supervisor about frequently getting back from lunch a couple minutes late. As it turned out, the supervisor was getting angry about it, but had not expressed it to Smitty. His supervisor was very appreciative that Smitty brought it up on his own. Smitty's more careful observation of his supervisor's body language may have saved his job.

SUMMARY OF CHAPTER 6: Attending to Facial Expressions

1. People all over the world have very similar basic facial expressions.
2. Upward expressions suggest positive and downward negative emotions.
3. Facial expressions can become sculpted permanently into the face.
4. Eye muscles are better indicators of emotions than mouth muscles.
5. Larger pupils suggest interest; staring suggests more intensity of emotion.
6. Genuine smiles have an upward pull of eye and mouth muscles.
7. An open mouth while listening sometimes suggests difficulty taking things in.
8. Relaxed exposure of the neck can signal comfort and receptivity.
9. Sighs suggest trying to accept something emotionally challenging.
10. Consider the overall situation along with gestures, voice, and speech.

CHAPTER 7
ATTENDING TO VOICE

 Attending to voice refers to listening to voice tone, volume, rate, and style as indicators of thoughts and feelings.

1. After attending to gestures and facial expressions, the next type of behavior to attend to concerns verbal communication expressed in the voice. Variations in voice tone, volume, rate of speech, accents, and style of speech reflect changes in inner thoughts and feelings. When people are speaking naturally and in an assertively balanced way, their voices fluctuate with the feelings and thoughts being expressed. These natural variations make speech more lively and interesting, and also convey meaning to careful listeners.

2. When the voice is smooth and easy to listen to, it suggests an assertive style of feeling relaxed and enjoying communicating. When the voice is shaky or speech is fast, it sometimes suggests anxiousness associated more with non-assertiveness. However, on occasion, speaking fast can indicate enthusiasm, or even anger. When you hear these styles of voice, help the person settle down by asking in a kind manner to repeat what was said so you are sure to understand, because what they are saying will likely give you good information about the person's thoughts and feelings.

3. When the voice is very quiet or soft, it suggests a non-assertive, anxious, and withdrawn style. But when the voice is very breathy with too much air, it frequently suggests being overly dramatic with expressions of feeling, or even artificial and manipulative in a passive-aggressive style.

4. When the volume or loudness of the voice increases, it usually indicates more excitement and intensity of feeling. Typically the pitch or tone of voice becomes higher and the rate of speech increases. These can indicate positive or negative excitement. On the other hand, volume and tone frequently get lower, and the rate decreases, when a person is tired or feeling down.

5. When the voice is harsh, shrill, and very penetrating, it usually suggests negative excitement that may signal danger, associated with non-assertive anxiety and fear or aggressive anger.

6. Frequently people will try to tell you what is important by accenting certain words. Accented words are spoken a little louder and with more verbal energy. Accented words tend to contain more information about thoughts and feelings than the overall speech content. When people pause between words in an awkward way that makes it a little more difficult to understand their meaning, or they place accents on words that don't seem appropriate given what is being said, it suggests being confused or distracted. Sometimes unusual accenting is due to cultural differences, but it could be due to confusion. Asking for clarification can be helpful.

7. When people talk in an aggressive, harsh, angry style, it is easy to allow your own verbal responses to get louder and more intense. This tends to make the situation worse. The tone of your voice and the loudness of your speech can sometimes make the difference between things cooling down or escalating further. Even if others get louder, keep speaking at about the same volume and tone you normally speak, and don't try to shout to get through to them. For the most part, avoid yelling, trying to instruct, or insisting in a firm voice at that time. Usually calmness and extra courtesy reduce negative emotions, not more voice volume.

8. When the voice style is inconsistent with the content of the speech and meaning of the words, it suggests that there is lack of coordination between what is being said and the underlying thoughts and feelings. For example, people may talk about an emergency, but in a monotonous style suggesting boredom. The bodily signals, voice style and tone, and content of speech should match, be consistent or congruent with each other. If this doesn't seem to be the case, then it is a good time to ask for clarification and listen carefully, in order to get more consistent information.

9. Other signals can help distinguish between positive and negative emotions related to changes in voice volume and tone, including body language, speech, and the overall context of what is going on at that time. Cultural influences also affect these qualities of voice and need to be understood in order to interpret inner thoughts and feelings.

10. In general, there are three basic questions to be answered in attending to voice:

    A. Normal or loud and fast?

    B. Steady or shaky?

    C. Relaxed or tight?

Examples of How to Use This Skill

EXAMPLE 1

Ineffective use: As Chip walked up to the counter in a restaurant and asked to look at the menu, the waitress asked if he wanted to sit down and have lunch. Chip said again that he wanted to look at the menu, raising his voice a bit. The waitress replied, 'Well, O.K., but would you stand out of the way so other customers can be seated.' Not seeing that someone was trying to walk around him at that moment, Chip considered her reply and tone to be a bit harsh, and commented on it. When the waitress said the menu is posted on the wall outside and walked away, Chip decided to try another restaurant.

Effective use: When Chip asked to see a menu he noticed that the waitress was quite busy, and that she might be a bit abrupt in her interactions. He said that he had never been to the restaurant before and wanted to look at the menu before being seated. The waitress said he could look at the menu posted in the entry way, or she would bring him one in a minute. He said thanks and that he would wait for her to bring a menu.

EXAMPLE 2

Ineffective use: On vacation in Montana with his mother, Ed wanted to take a beautiful high mountain drive that was somewhat dangerous due to the narrow road and deep valleys. Ed's mother paused a moment, said that whatever he wanted to do was fine, but also said that she might possibly want to stop at the gift shop she heard about the day before. As they started out on the high mountain road, his mother became increasingly nervous and quiet. Ed assumed that she was just not feeling well, maybe due to all the driving they had been doing on the vacation, not realizing his mother was trying to tell him she was hesitant about the high mountain drive.

Effective use: When Brian asked his young boy, Cody, to go on the jungle ride with him to see the wild animals, Cody nodded his head yes. But when Brian walked over to get in line, Cody hesitated, stood where he was, and then in an excited way said he was hungry. When Brian said they would eat right after going on the ride, Cody then said he had to go to the bathroom. Brian began to wonder whether there was something about the jungle ride that might be frightening to Cody. In a quiet and slow voice, Cody responded that he wasn't afraid, but just didn't want to do it now. Brian decided other priorities might be more important than the jungle ride, and said to Cody that the bathroom was close to the snack bar. Later he would talk to Cody about what he thought the jungle ride would be like and perhaps clarify it.

EXAMPLE 3

Ineffective use: When little Jimmy came into the classroom, he was talking very fast and in a high pitched tone. Mrs. Ellis, his second grade teacher, immediately saw that Jimmy was overly excited and told him to quiet down because other kids were already in their seats starting to draw. Jimmy began whimpering. When he was again told to sit down, he started crying.

Effective use: As little Jimmy came into class, Mrs. Ellis noticed that he was talking louder and faster than usual. She asked him if things were okay, and he began to explain in a shaky voice how a car had screeched to a stop in front of him when he was walking to school. Mrs. Ellis sat by him a minute and listened as he described the incident. Soon he began to relax, and then he pulled out his drawing supplies and started drawing on his own, even without having to be told what to do.

SUMMARY OF CHAPTER 7: Attending to Voice

1. Voice tone, volume, rate, and style contain helpful clues.
2. Shaky or fast speaking suggests nervousness and non-assertiveness.
3. Very soft voice tone suggests non-assertiveness.
4. Loud or high-pitched voice suggests strong feelings.
5. Shrill, penetrating voice suggests negative excitement such as fear.
6. Accented words signal important content.
7. Be alert to how your voice style is affecting other people.
8. If voice is not consistent with other indicators, get more clarification.
9. Consider body language, speech, and the overall situation.
10. Key voice issues are: normal/loud and fast; relaxed/tight; steady/shaky.

CHAPTER 8
ATTENDING TO SPEECH

 Attending to speech refers to listening to specific words and phrases as indicators of thoughts and feelings.

1. In addition to attending to body language and voice, carefully listening to specific words and phrases people use in speech provides useful information that may otherwise be overlooked. Words or phrases that are repeated, used in unusual ways, or emphasized with more volume or deliberateness are examples of speech that very likely includes more information about inner thoughts and feelings. Identifying thoughts and feelings reflected in speech requires careful listening.

2. If people are sensitive about taking the risk to express certain thoughts and feelings, they may have difficulty putting them into words. When this occurs, the information may be important. It is helpful to be patient and stay on the topic to support their attempts to express challenging thoughts and feelings. Showing frustration, impatience, disinterest, or changing the topic can result in losing a rare chance to communicate more deeply. If people are reluctant to tell you something, it is usually effective to listen more carefully and patiently. But this doesn't mean pressuring them to talk about it.

3. People usually want to communicate, even if it is initially difficult. It is even common for people to answer a question in a few minutes that they were at first not willing or able to answer. The answer may not be obvious, and it may be hidden in other information; but frequently it will be present in their speech within a couple minutes. If you first tell people they don't have to answer if they don't want, it sometimes increases the likelihood they will answer after a short time. It also can be helpful to ask the question again after talking a while, but in an inviting rather than insisting manner. This frequently results in getting the answer, or at least useful related information.

4. People sometimes give information about their thoughts and feelings by repeating key words or phrases, or by using words in unusual ways. For example, a person may find it hard to express fear about something, but may refer to frightening experiences in the news, without ever bringing up their own fear. They also may use terms that refer to fear even though the content of their speech and other clues may not clearly or directly suggest fear.

5. Sometimes people have speech styles that reflect characteristic patterns of thoughts and feelings. Listening for even a few minutes may reveal the pattern. For example, use of very few words or brief bursts of words suggest non-assertiveness. Harsh, critical speech suggests aggressive emotions. Use of many words that run on without breaks, or with vague or elaborate descriptions, also suggests a non-assertive

style. In a general way, 'I don't know' tends toward meaning 'no;' and 'I don't care' tends toward meaning 'yes' or 'okay.'

6. The actual words we use can have a significant effect on our own experience, as well as how others interpret our thoughts and feelings. Specific words can have specific effects. For example, using the word scary to describe parachuting can create quite a different impression than the word exciting. If the meaning is not clear, it is important to ask.

7. It is beneficial in your own speech to help the listener understand by using precise descriptions, such as saying that rock climbing was too dangerous rather than intense. Using more than one descriptor, such as adding the words uncomfortable or upsetting, also provides more clarity. An important example of how specific speech expressions have different effects is in giving feedback. It's easier to accept statements such as, 'Your answer was incomplete,' or, 'Your behavior is not acceptable,' than, 'You were wrong,' or, 'You are unacceptable.'

8. Frequently people will place emphasis on a particular word that changes the overall meaning of the statement. This may involve increased or decreased volume, speaking slower and more deliberately, pausing before saying something, or adding body language such as a gesture or a facial expression. These provide strong clues of the underlying thoughts and feelings. Any change in speech style during a statement is likely to convey additional meaning.

9. For example, a statement may be about being late, but the emphasis indicates emotions of frustration and impatience, such as, 'You weren't that late for the meeting.' A statement about appearance might include a meaningful addition such as, 'Well! You sure look nice today;' suggesting interest in the reason for dressing up. When people talk in an indirect style, ask for clarification. Such indirect messages sometimes reflect negative and aggressive emotions, but also sometimes can indicate playfulness and teasing.

10. In listening to speech style, it is important whether the rate of speech is normal, associated with relaxed emotions and balanced assertiveness; or fast, associated with a more tense state, perhaps of anxiety, anger, or excitement. Also, emphasized words help in understanding thoughts and feelings that are not being directly expressed.

Examples of How to Use This Skill

EXAMPLE 1

Ineffective use: When Janet asked her new boyfriend, Craig, about deep sea fishing, Craig described his one childhood experience of it as 'different and pretty exciting.' From this somewhat vague description, Janet thought Craig might like to do it again, so she arranged for a half-day fishing excursion for Craig's birthday. When she told Craig about it, he was not enthusiastic and really didn't want to do it. He explained that on his childhood trip, he actually got sea sick and almost fell off the boat into the choppy waters, which he remembered as quite scary. Janet felt like her idea was rejected, and she decided not even to try arranging something special for his birthday after she had to cancel the boat trip and forfeit the deposit.

Effective use: Because from her boyfriend's comments in a conversation about deep sea fishing she was not able to tell whether he enjoyed it or not, Janet decided to ask him more about it to get a better understanding. When he described it further as somewhat of a traumatic experience for him, it became clear that it would not be a good option for a birthday surprise. She ended up getting tickets for a ball game which she was more certain he would like. They had a great time together at the game, and he thanked her several times.

EXAMPLE 2

Ineffective use: When Rod's teenage daughter, Maria, came into the den, Rod asked her if she wanted to watch the championship soccer match on TV with him. Maria didn't immediately respond, and Rod asked again in a different way. Maria said she didn't know, and then mumbled something about not feeling right that didn't quite make sense to Rod, who at the same time was trying to follow the game. Rod said that she should speak up and say what she felt, and it was frustrating when she was so wishy-washy. Maria started to sob a little, and said she was going to her room. Rod thought she was in one of her typical moods, and went back to watching TV.

Effective use: When Rod noticed a somewhat unusual response from his daughter that didn't quite make sense, he looked at her directly, and asked if she was feeling okay. After a while, Maria said she had a headache and felt a little confused. As Rod attended more to her, she said that she may have hit her head when she fell out of bed, but she wasn't sure what happened. Rod called his wife back from the neighbor's house and they decided to take Maria to the doctor's office to check on a possible concussion.

EXAMPLE 3

Ineffective use: Ross was sure his boss would be quite upset if she saw the spelling mistake in the new ad; and he was concerned about getting fired. He was offered another job recently, but had to commit by Friday, so he needed to find out his status right away. When his boss came in, she was talking loudly to the secretary about how things are frustrating and out of control in the office. Ross assumed it was about the mistake in the ad, and felt it best not to deal with it but rather just to go call about the other job.

Effective use: Carol, the secretary, also was concerned about a mistake of sending a letter to the wrong person, but decided to find out first what was upsetting her boss. She knew her boss had a check-up this morning, and asked how it went. Her boss confided that more tests were needed, which scared her a little. Carol postponed bringing up the mistake, and asked how she could be helpful. The boss appreciated her support. Later Carol bought up her mistake when the time seemed appropriate, and she and her boss discussed how to reduce the chance of this type of mistake occurring again.

SUMMARY OF CHAPTER 8: Attending to Speech

1. Careful listening to speech can provide clues otherwise overlooked.
2. If people hesitate about something, it indicates it may be important.
3. People usually answer questions they are first hesitant to answer.
4. People frequently repeat important words or phrases as signals.
5. Styles of speech sometimes reveal emotional patterns.
6. Precise descriptions help clarify inner thoughts and feelings.
7. Use words that precisely describe your thoughts and feelings.
8. Any change in style in a statement may be an important signal.
9. Listen for words that indirectly signal emotional content.
10. A basic question is whether the rate of speech is normal or fast.

Putting It All Together

Attending Skills

Attending skills will help you learn to be more observant in communicating with other people. They can be put together into a sequence to develop an effective approach to listening. First attend to gestures and facial expressions, and then voice and speech styles.

With non-verbal behavior, open and relaxed gestures, orienting toward the other person, and upward facial expressions suggest positive thoughts and feelings and assertive interest. The opposite features suggest negative thoughts and feelings such as non-assertiveness and defensiveness. When attending to non-verbal behavior, consider these points:

- Posture open or closed?
- Movement relaxed or rigid?
- Gestures toward you or away?
- Facial expressions upward or downward?

With respect to verbal behavior, normal loudness, relaxed tone, steadiness, and normal rate of speech suggest positive thoughts and feelings, and assertive interest. The opposite features suggest negative thoughts and feelings. When attending to verbal behavior, consider these points:

- Voice style steady or shaky?
- Voice volume normal or loud?
- Voice tone relaxed or tight?
- Speech rate normal or fast?

Gestures and facial expressions, voice tone and style, and the content and meaning of speech all need to be congruent. This means that they need to fit with, match, or be consistent each other. They need to point in the same general direction of identifying what may be going on in a person's heart and mind. If this is not the case, then mixed messages are being sent. Under these circumstances, attend and listen very carefully for more clarity, and ask for more information.

ENGAGING SKILLS

Once you have attended to the outermost signals of communication such as postures and speech style, then use skills that promote further the exchange of thoughts and feelings. These skills are used to engage people more fully in the communication process, especially by listening very carefully. Careful observing and listening are fundamental to healthy, effective communication.

Engaging skills are basic communication skills that help initiate and maintain verbal communication with other people. The chapters in this category include listening, prompting, questioning, and matching.

CHAPTER 9
LISTENING

 Listening refers to openly using senses, mind, and heart to receive what other people are saying without distraction.

1. In addition to attending to body language and speech, effective communication involves careful listening. It has been said that God gave us two ears and one mouth to remind us to listen twice as much as we talk. Listening is the key to healthy communication. It is a very important skill that involves assertive balance, alertness, patience, and respect for yourself and others. It requires a lot of practice to develop and refine.

2. A basic principle of communication is to understand others before trying to get them to understand you. In large part, miscommunication is due to trying to make others understand you before you understand them. You will be much more effective by listening first. People will be more willing to listen to you after they have been heard. Many of the tools in this book encourage listening first. Of course there are situations when it may be necessary to speak first, especially in emergencies when you have knowledge that will protect others. However, even in times of crisis it frequently helps to be informed by listening in order to determine the appropriate action to take.

3. Listening is one of the best ways to learn things quickly. You will have better information for making an appropriate reply, and can thus avoid a rash and uninformed response. In the long run, listening will save you time and energy. It pays to pay attention and listen before speaking.

4. The inner mechanics of listening involve taking in information without trying to prepare a response at the same time. If you're trying to figure out a response while people are talking to you, your attention will be divided and it will be difficult to receive the information clearly and reply appropriately. It is harder to listen when you are thinking about something else, such as trying to figure out how you will respond, or comparing yourself to others, or looking for mistakes or faults in what others are saying.

5. As noted in an earlier chapter, the human information processing system can be likened to the central processor of a computer that processes one thing at a time—either input or output. A basic principle of communication is to receive input fully before attempting output. Listening involves receiving input and processing it so it is understood, prior to giving output. In this process, parts of the mind and heart needed for an effective response are activated, which makes deciding on a response easier.

6. It is not effective to force an impulsive response before understanding the situation. Asserting your own goals and plans is more difficult if the necessary parts of your mind and heart are not activated that guides action to fit the circumstances. When this happens, non-assertive hesitation about how to respond or an aggressive, impulsive response can result. These are indicators to assert yourself by first asking and then listening more carefully. People will appreciate your interest in what they have to say.

7. Respond to issues you understand, and postpone immediately responding to issues about which you aren't clear. When you're not clear about how to respond, the assertive response is to say that the person deserves a well-thought-out reply and you will respond after thinking about it. Sometimes listening involves taking time to reflect on what was said before deciding on a reply. Assertive listening includes the ability to ask for time to think things through before responding. However, thinking but not acting produces non-assertiveness. Take the available time to think it through, but then give a timely reply based on your best understanding of the situation.

8. Listening doesn't mean forcing yourself to pay attention. Straining wastes energy, produces more inner noise, and reduces ability to receive information. Attention naturally flows toward something more enjoyable. Listening involves allowing attention to be drawn to deeper levels of what is being said. These deeper levels of communication are naturally more enjoyable. Forcing and straining lock attention on superficial levels of experience, which quickly gets boring.

9. For example, let's say you want to give quality time to your daughter, but find it hard to pay attention. The experience is not charming. This may be due to you being tired, or inadequate planning such as poor timing, or a distracting environment, or activities that are not engaging to you and your child. Generally it is not that attending to your child is inherently a struggle and you must suffer through it to be a good parent. It rather may be that rest and proper planning is needed to engage your creativity and flexibility to identify experiences that you and your daughter will both enjoy together.

10. The skill of listening involves being more settled in your heart and mind. When inner noise is reduced and inner silence increases, it is easier to listen. Mental processes involved in listening become more efficient in processing incoming information. The levels of mind and heart that produce balanced, assertive responses are more naturally and fully activated, allowing more powerful and effective expression of feelings and thoughts.

Examples of How to Use This Skill

EXAMPLE 1

Ineffective use: While Ashley was listening to Jill talk about the party last weekend, she happened to overhear another friend mention Rick's name, and Ashley is very interested in Rick. Ashley wanted to hear what Jill was saying and tried to pay attention, but was distracted by the conversation about Rick. Jill noticed Asley wasn't really listening, finally got mad and said that Ashley didn't really care about what Jill was trying to tell her.

Effective use: When Ashley heard her friends talking about Rick, she immediately asked Jill if she could briefly listen to the other conversation. She really wanted to hear about the party, but knew she'd be distracted and couldn't give Jill her full attention. Jill agreed to walk back to class with Ashley and finish her story about the party.

EXAMPLE 2

Ineffective use: When Sarah overheard her sister, Sheila, say that she was considering moving into the room after their brother leaves for college, Sarah became very angry and began yelling at Sheila, saying that she always butts in and disrupts Sarah's plans. Sheila had no clue what triggered Sarah's attack, and began yelling back at her for being so emotional and difficult.

Effective use: When Sarah heard her sister, Sheila, talking on the phone to a friend about moving, she wondered if it related to her own plans to take over their brother's room when he goes to college. After her sister got off the phone, Sarah asked her about it. Sheila explained that she has been considering fixing up and moving into the small room above the garage, and that it sounded like fun to decorate her own little place. Then Sarah understood that her sister was not planning at all to move into their brother's room. Sheila said she had no plans to do that, because she knew Sarah already had first choice on it.

EXAMPLE 3

Ineffective use: In a company board meeting, Jeff was asked by the chairperson about a detailed point in accounting. But Jeff wasn't sure from the way it was asked whether the chairperson asked about the core issue. The question was asked in a way to suggest that Jeff should support the chairperson's view of the situation under discussion. Without feeling confident about it, Jeff gives a general answer that the chairperson takes to mean is in support of his own understanding. Later, Jeff is concerned that his answer could lead to a misunderstanding on the part of the board members.

Effective use: In a board meeting, Jeff feels pressure to give a response, but is not certain that it will actually clarify the issue under discussion, even though it might support the chairperson. He asserts himself by saying that the issue requires a detailed explanation, and asks if he should take the time to discuss it more right now, or research it further and present it later in a memo, later in the meeting, or at another meeting. The chairperson asks Jeff if he actually knows the answer. Jeff says yes, but also explains that there are two parts to the question. Jeff skillfully deals with the issue, providing accurate information, but also supporting the chairperson.

SUMMARY OF CHAPTER 9: Listening

1. Listening is the key to effective communication.
2. Understand others first before trying to be understood.
3. Careful listening fosters rapid learning.
4. It is important to listen fully before trying to respond.
5. Listening activates heart and mind for more effective responding.
6. Impulsive reacting before understanding creates miscommunication.
7. Assert yourself by asking for more time to think if needed.
8. Listening doesn't mean forced effort to pay attention.
9. Difficulty listening is usually due to tiredness or improper planning.
10. Reducing inner noise helps mind and heart work better in listening.

CHAPTER 10
PROMPTING

 Prompting refers to applying verbal and non-verbal behavior that encourages people to communicate.

1. Communication not only involves observing people and listening to what they are saying, but also actively fostering communication. There is a time to stop talking and start doing, but there is also a time to talk. It is helpful to know how to keep a conversation going when it is time to talk. Some actions encourage communication, whereas others make it more difficult.

2. A block to communication is a style of speaking or other behavior that interferes with communication and discourages continuing a conversation. If you find that communication with certain people tends to be difficult, consider whether you are displaying some of the common blocks to communication. Generally they are associated with non-assertive hesitation or aggressive defensiveness or attack.

3. Examples of non-verbal behaviors that block communication include intruding on people's personal space such as standing too close or over them, touching people when it is uncomfortable for them, staring or looking away, ignoring, showing restlessness, crossing arms over the chest, jerky or quick body movements, or displaying facial expressions that suggest disapproval, impatience, boredom, or sleepiness.

4. Examples of verbal behaviors that block communication include talking too loud or too soft, yelling, interrupting, speaking harshly or too fast, being bossy, criticizing, blaming, being sarcastic and a bit rude, giving advice unasked, threatening verbally, lecturing or preaching, using words people don't understand, using the same words or phrases over and over again, persisting too long on a topic, not pausing to give others a chance to talk, and saying one thing but thinking and feeling something else.

5. The communication skill of prompting basically involves avoiding blocks to communication and giving encouraging signals to people to show you want to hear what they are saying. Non-verbal prompts or encouragers are gestures and body language that signal you are listening and that reinforce communication. They include such signals as smiling, making eye contact, looking at the person and waiting for him or her to speak, leaning toward the person, and an easy, relaxed, but alert body posture.

6. Verbal prompts or encouragers are brief verbal reactions you can insert into a conversation that signal you are listening and that reinforce talking behavior in others. They include such statements as, 'Hmm, a huh, yes, and, really, okay, and then what, wow, no kidding, that's great, nice, you don't say, that's interesting, I didn't know that, I'm glad you told me that, or please tell me more about....' Laughing is

also a powerful signal that usually fosters communication. In addition, moments of silence to think about things can foster communication. Using peoples' names also is helpful to promote conversation, such as saying something like, 'That's interesting, Jerry!'

7. Questioning can also be an excellent way to prompt more communication. It not only helps introduce new topics, but also allows people to go further into a topic by helping them focus more deeply on it. Questioning is probably the best way to keep conversations going with people you don't know very well. If you want people to talk to you more, question them about themselves. Questions about their opinions or what they enjoy doing are usually effective. It is helpful to focus on the immediate circumstances to find things to ask. Refer to the upcoming chapter on questioning for more details.

8. Personal questions need to be asked with care and sensitivity. It is usually helpful to start with an introductory statement such as, 'If you feel comfortable talking about this, I'd like to know about...' or, 'Please let me know if you don't want to talk about ... but I would be interested in your answer to ...' Watch for body language or speech signals indicating increased tension, and explore changing the topic if they occur.

9. Techniques that involve saying back what others have said, such as summarizing, are also useful ways to foster communication. Summarizing involves restating what others have just said to you. It shows you are listening and want others to continue talking. A subtle tool that fosters communication is called matching language. This involves using the same words or examples that others use in their speech. For example, use words related to gardening, a sport, or their career if these are the topics they are discussing. Refer to the upcoming chapters on summarizing and matching language for more information on these skills.

10. Use of prompting demonstrates your interest in other people and willingness to learn about them. The more you are able to tune in to other people's thoughts and feelings, the more they will see you as a good communicator and will want to talk with you. Many people in our society today are emotionally starving to be listened to, validated, and accepted. Your communication will be valued and appreciated by other people if you develop the skills to foster these experiences.

Examples of How to Use This Skill

EXAMPLE 1

Ineffective use: Allen was very interested in what Shirley was talking about, and couldn't wait to add his own ideas. Allen liked Shirley and wanted to show that he had similar interests. As soon as she finished what seemed like a sentence, Allen quickly jumped in and said, 'I know what you mean,' and then tried to further her point. After a while, Shirley backed off and was less interested in talking, which confused Allen.

Effective use: Allen decided to ask Shirley the reason she seemed to lose interest in the topic. She said she didn't lose interest, but found it hard to continue when Allen kept butting in with what he wanted to say. Allen asked if Shirley would explain more, because he wanted to learn how to communicate more effectively. While Shirley talked about it, Allen carefully listened. After a while, Shirley asked him what he thought, and Allen was able to respond very well after understanding her explanation. From then on, the conversation went smoothly and Shirley even began talking about the original topic again.

EXAMPLE 2

Ineffective use: Each time Shepley's son asked why something is like it is, or how things work, Shepley used examples from his own computer software engineering work. Because his young son was confused about computers and didn't like them because they took away his father's attention all the time, his son quickly tuned out when Shepley tried to explain things with computer analogies. Shepley began showing impatience when his son asked questions.

Effective use: When Shepley's son asked questions to him, Shepley learned to ask questions to his son to clarify his son's thinking. He also began to use examples that fit into his son's interests—Lego sets and basketball—and not to use examples from his specialty of computer science, with which his son seemed to have little interest, or at least little comfort.

EXAMPLE 3

Ineffective use: Shepley thought that the best way to listen to others at work, especially complicated engineering concepts, was to look at them and pay attention, without interrupting in any way. When he just stared at people who were talking to him, however, he found over time that people seemed not to engage in deeper conversations with him. He began to feel left out of much of the communication that went on between his co-workers in the office.

Effective use: One day Shepley stopped in the office of the personnel director to discuss with him his growing feeling of isolation in the office. In the discussion, the personnel director mentioned that Shepley actually was gaining the reputation of a person who seemed not to be interested or involved in what other people tried to talk to him about. They discussed ways Shepley could demonstrate more effectively that he was engaged in the communication with others by giving acknowledgement during the conversations.

SUMMARY OF CHAPTER 10: Prompting

1. Certain verbal and non-verbal behaviors encourage communication.
2. Non-assertive and aggressive behaviors block communication.
3. Non-verbal blocks include staring, looking away, and crossing arms.
4. Verbal blocks include talking too loud or soft, and interrupting.
5. Non-verbal and verbal prompting encourages conversation.
6. Verbal prompts include 'hmm, ahuh, yes, then what, tell me more.'
7. Use questioning to start or get deeper into a topic.
8. Change the topic quickly if people show signs of discomfort.
9. Use the same language and examples other people are using.
10. Many people are emotionally starved to be listened to and accepted.

CHAPTER 11
QUESTIONING

 Questioning refers to getting more information or clarifying the meaning of what other people are saying by asking about it.

1. Along with prompting, a useful part of fostering communication is effective questioning. You have probably had the pleasant experience of finding people who are especially interesting to talk with and who seem to communicate with you better than other people do. It is likely they showed real interest in your life, and showed it by asking questions about you. Knowing how to ask questions in a way that fosters communication will help other people see you as an effective communicator. Asking questions is an excellent way to show people you are interested in them. Of course, asking questions needs to be followed by attentively listening to the answer.

2. Questioning is an information-gathering technique useful for improving your understanding of others' thoughts and feelings. It also helps get to the point more quickly and more clearly. Two major types of questions are closed and open questions.

3. A closed question is a question that is worded to produce a short, specific answer such as a simple 'yes' or 'no.' Here are some examples of closed questions: 'Do you like tennis?' 'Are you ready now?' 'Do you want to stop for lunch at Noon or at 1:00?' 'How long will you be on vacation?' 'Is Debbie at the office or in her truck?'

4. Closed questions provide specific information. They tend to guide people away from complicated answers, and thus can make communication simpler. Closed questions can be very helpful in communicating with someone who is non-assertive, scared, confused, or reluctant to talk. However, people who are aggressive, irritated, and angry could become even more upset by the restrictive nature of closed questions. In such cases, it helps to ask if they want specific questions or want to explain things more.

5. Open questions are questions that are worded to produce more elaborate answers and explanations. They are designed to give people the opportunity to talk more about what they are thinking and feeling. This type of question frequently includes a request for the person to explain what or how. Here are some examples of open questions: 'What do you feel about extreme sports?' 'What is your opinion about that artistic style?' 'How is that done?' 'How come we have to pay taxes?' 'What do you think about it?'

6. Asking open questions is the key to establishing deeper communication, such as, for example, to someone you want to get to know more. Most people like to talk about themselves when someone actually shows interest. However, because people tend to reveal more of their feelings when asked open questions, it is important that the open questions not probe private information that they may not yet want to reveal. An open question such as, 'Where do you like to go for vacation?' or 'Would you tell me more about your musical tastes?' allow other people to decide how much detail to provided and what direction to take the conversation. Closed questions such as 'How old are you?' or, 'Have you been to a spa lately?' are more restrictive, can be too personal, and make conversing more difficult by not encouraging discussion.

7. Very generally, closed questions are used to tap thoughts in the mind; they deal with specifics. Open questions are used to tap feelings in the heart; they deal more with openness of communication.

8. Combining both closed and open questions is effective to get specific information and also foster communication. Generally, use open questions to get a general understanding of what others want to talk about, and use closed questions to clarify specific information. The overall situation will be a guide as to when open or closed questions are appropriate.

9. Sometimes people speak in vague, general ways that don't provide clear information. Closed questions are useful on these occasions. For example, a person might say, 'It might be nice if you wanted me to spend time with you this weekend.' There are several possible meanings to this statement. For example, it might mean that the person feels ignored, or that the person does not want to spend time with you right now, or that the person wants a date with you, or that the person is pushing to get involved with you. Clear questions such as, 'Do you want me to ask you over for lunch?' or, 'Do you feel frustrated because I haven't spent time with you?' help clarify the thoughts and feelings that are behind the person's unclear statement.

10. It is important for healthy, effective communication to ask specific questions to clarify the meaning, before you assert your own thoughts and feelings. Otherwise, your response may be interpreted in a completely different way than you intended. For example, if your reply to the above vague statement was just, 'Okay,' you might find the person pushing to stay for the weekend, when you thought you were just acknowledging the person's interest in spending a little more time with you.

Examples of How to Use This Skill

EXAMPLE 1

Ineffective use: Phil is standing next to Marilyn, wants to find out who she is, and decides to talk with her. He starts by saying, 'Hi, where do you live?' Marilyn cautiously responds, 'In town.' Phil asks, 'Do you plan to stay for the whole meeting?' Marilyn more cautiously says, 'I'm not sure yet.' Phil continues with more questions, 'Did you like that last speaker? What did you think about her point about morality in the movies?' Finally, Marilyn says, 'Would you excuse me? I see someone I need to talk with.'

Effective use: Phil wants to meet the lady standing by him. He says: 'Hi! I'm from Butte County. Mind if I introduce myself while we're waiting for the next speaker?' Marilyn gives an acknowledging smile. Phil continues, 'I'm Phil Jenkins, one of the Butte County delegates.' She replies, 'Hi. I'm Marilyn Lemsky.' Phil says: 'That last speaker seemed to get peoples' attention; may I ask what your reaction was to her speech?' Phil and Marilyn have an enjoyable conversation for the next five minutes.

EXAMPLE 2

Ineffective use: The first time Jan and Ted bring up to their children plans for summer vacation this year, Ted says, 'Do you want to go to Grandpa's or to Aunt Donna's for vacation this year?' The children don't seem responsive, and when asked again say, 'I don't know.' Jan and Ted both are a little frustrated by their children's indecisiveness and unenthusiastic response.

Effective use: The first time Jan and Ted bring up to their children the topic of vacation, Jan says, 'Our vacation time again this year is the last two weeks of July. Have you had any ideas on where you might like to go this year?' The kids all say no, and then Jan asks, 'What do you think of coming up with a wish list of suggestions, then next week we can talk again about it and narrow down the possibilities?' With a little more enthusiasm, the children agree to think about it.

EXAMPLE 3

Ineffective use: Upon returning from a very informative and creative conference, Ilana stops by the office of her boss, wanting to tell the boss about her new ideas. Her boss first asks, 'Are you back now? How many days were you gone this time? Was it productive?' 'Are any other conferences scheduled for this calendar year?' 'When's the next one, and where will it be?' Right away much of Ilana's enthusiasm is dissipated and she leaves the office with no chance of sharing her new knowledge and creative ideas with her boss.

Effective use: When Ilana passes by her boss, she says, 'The conference was very productive, and I'd like 10 minutes to summarize the progress for you, and discuss some new ideas. Do you have time now, or would tomorrow after lunch be better?'

SUMMARY OF CHAPTER 11: Questioning

1. Questioning needs to be followed up with attentive listening.
2. There are two basic types of questions: closed and open.
3. Closed questions encourage short, specific, clear answers.
4. Closed questions are helpful with non-assertive or scared people.
5. Open questions encourage more elaborate explanations.
6. Open questions help connect to people you don't know.
7. Generally closed questions tap mind and open questions heart.
8. Use open questions for general and closed for specific information.
9. The purpose of questioning is clarity about thoughts and feelings.
10. Questioning helps avoid miscommunication.

CHAPTER 12
MATCHING

 Matching refers to listening to key words or phrases other people are using and then using the same words or language context in the conversation.

1. As you interact with other people using listening, prompting, and questioning skills, an excellent way to help people be more comfortable talking with you is to use some of the same words or phrases they use. This is called matching. This skill involves listening carefully to specific speech expressions used by other people and including some of them in your own speech. Sometimes people will accept that you understand them only if you use the same words they use to describe a concept important to them.

2. This doesn't mean copying peoples' style of speaking, but rather listening to the language expressions people use, and sometimes using the same words. For example, the statement, 'I hope I don't strike out with my dinner date tonight,' includes an expression from baseball. A matching reply might be, 'It might be better not to go for a homerun your first time up to the plate.'

3. Fad language is an example of how people develop more comfort with each other by using the same speech expressions. In the 1950s it was good to be cool or hip; in the 1960s it was good to be groovy or far out; in the 1970s it was good to be hot or bad; in the 1980s it was good to be rad or awesome; in the 1990s it was good to be sweet or way cool. In the 2000s, the terms seem to be cool or tight. It's interesting that cool has been in use for almost 75 years! Teenagers may relate more easily to a statement such as, 'That's a cool shirt,' than to, 'The shirt adorning your upper torso is very stylish in my humble opinion;' or to the statement, 'Do your own thing,' rather than, 'Man is endowed with certain inalienable rights.'

4. There are trends in language use among different groups of people. These trends may reflect sociocultural groups, age groups, ethnic groups, or gender differences. One theory of male-female differences is that females use more heart and feeling language and males use more mind and thinking language. Thus males will say, 'I don't think you understand,' and females will say, 'I feel like you don't understand.' This is consistent with the general idea that females tend to be oriented more toward heart and males more toward mind.

5. A related theory is that males tend to use more visual metaphors, and females tend to use more touch metaphors. Thus males tend to say, 'I don't see what you mean;' 'That doesn't look right;' or, 'The poem gave me a clear picture.' In contrast, females might tend more toward saying, 'I don't feel that way;' 'I am uncomfortable about that;' or, 'The poem touched me deeply.'

6. In the interesting ancient theory called Ayurveda, personality patterns including language styles reflect basic mind-body types. Thin people who tend to be quick-minded and anxious have more of a tendency to use hearing and touch metaphors. Athletic people who tend to be enthusiastic and more impatient tend more toward visual metaphors. Larger-framed, physically strong people who tend to be slower moving tend to use taste and smell metaphors. Thus people might say, 'It doesn't sound good;' or, 'It doesn't look right;' or, 'It smells funny or suspicious,' or, 'It leaves a bad taste in my mouth.'

7. Whether or not you agree with these theories, if you listen carefully you will notice that some people do use specific words and patterns of phrases more frequently than other people. Identifying and using key words, as well as the general language context other people use, can help communication.

8. For example, let's say someone tells you about their vacation in this way: 'Last year I went to Italy; the views were beautiful, especially the architecture in Florence and the picturesque Mediterranean coastline. Those spots are the prettiest places I've ever seen. The views of the countryside and the look on the cheerful faces of the people were really something to see.' The person may feel a little disconnected with you if your reply used different sense metaphors than visual metaphors, such as, 'That really sounds wonderful. Hearing the Italian language and tasting their hearty cuisine must have felt wonderful. Just hearing about it touches my heart.' Contrast that reply with one that matches language, such as this, 'You paint a beautiful picture of your trip. Do you have any photos I can see?'

9. You can connect better with people not only by using similar sense metaphors, but also using examples from their personal interests. Frequently the area of work a person is in provides useful metaphors and examples. Also, areas of personal experience such as hobbies, sports, types of pets, fixing a car, building a house, using a computer, or sewing a dress provide examples people can relate to more easily.

10. For example, a farmer might relate easier to, 'You reap what you sow;' or, 'Prettier than a dew drop on a rose;' than to, 'What goes around comes around,' or, 'she'll steal the show!' A stockbroker might relate more to, 'It could be a bull week,' rather than, 'Break a leg!' Matching requires careful listening to identify the language context. However, sometimes a common word develops a very specific meaning. It can be quite important to ask about the meaning if you are not sure how a particular word is being used.

Examples of How to Use This Skill

EXAMPLE 1

Ineffective use: While Steve is mowing the front lawn of his new house, some boys walk by. He says, 'Hey boys, what's happening? You guys live around here?' One boy says, 'What's with all the questions?' Steve says, 'I just moved here and wanted to know who...' One of the boys interrupts and blurts out, 'Hey man, we didn't break your garage window.' Steve says, 'I'm just trying to be friendly, is that okay?' 'That ain't friendly, interrogating us like some kind of detective or something; chill out, man!' Steve replies: 'I think you need to chill out, man; or I should say, boy!'

Effective use: Steve says: 'Hey, men; got a second? I just moved in and want to find out what's around the neighborhood.' One boy says, 'You from Nebraska, like your license plate?' Steve replies, 'Yeah, a small town in western Nebraska.' The boy says, 'What's it like for you to live in civilization now (everyone laughs)?' Steve replies, 'Civilization sounds fun; where is it around here?' Another boy says, 'Lakeside Park is a mile that way; it has a big swimming pool and lots of sports. Why'd you move here?' Steve says, 'To work in the office for the White Sox.' A boy blurts out: 'Can you sneak us into a game? Steve says: 'I can get a few free passes. You guys like baseball?'

EXAMPLE 2

Ineffective use: Trying to understand and connect better with women, Ken decides to try out a new communication skill with his sister. When his sister walks into the living room and says, 'I haven't felt good all evening, and nothing on TV is very interesting. I can't relate at all to that new reality show,' Ken replies, 'I feel your pain.' His sister responds, 'Oh, did you eat some of the leftover pizza too? It wasn't very good even last weekend when it was fresh.'

Effective use: Trying out a new communication skill, when Ken's sister remarked that the special world news report on improved relations between North and South was very touching and powerful, Ken followed up with the comment, 'It gave me a good feel for the progress, after years of isolation on the part of both regions.' His sister sat down to talk more with Ken, and he was able to tune in further to the language context that she tends to use in her conversations.

EXAMPLE 3

Ineffective use: When Justin came back out to the warehouse, he was quite angry about what the company manager had said, and blurted out to his co-worker, Sam, 'That idiot yelled at me and didn't even have the guts to take the time to see my side of the picture; what a jerk.' Sam commented, 'I feel like this whole stinking company is run by jerks that don't care at all about us regular workers.'

Effective use: When Justin came back angry, Sam said, 'I'd like to get the picture of what happened, if you want to talk more about it.'

SUMMARY OF CHAPTER 12: Matching
1. The first step in matching is to listen for specific expressions.
2. Matching uses the same general context of other peoples' speech.
3. Fad language is a good example of the principle behind matching.
4. Males use mind and thinking language, women use heart and feeling.
5. Males tend to use visual metaphors and females use touch metaphors.
6. Sometimes language style can be related to peoples' mind-body types.
7. Identifying key words and the general context of speech is helpful.
8. People sometimes use examples that emphasize a particular sense.
9. Areas of work or personal interests provide excellent metaphors.
10. Matching requires knowledge of special word meanings.

Putting It All Together

Attending and Engaging Skills

Engaging skills basically will help you listen more carefully and become more tuned in when you are interacting with other people. They add to attending skills in the sequence of outer to inner levels of effective communication by beginning to get more engaged or involved in the process of communicating. First attend to gestures and facial expressions, then voice and speech styles, and then use engaging skills to foster additional verbal communication.

The most important engaging skill is listening, and the key to listening is to pay attention in order to take into your mind what the other person is saying. If you are sincerely listening, your own body postures and voice qualities will be congruent and naturally reflect your willingness to communicate. There are many degrees or levels of depth of listening, from observing obvious outer levels to the subtle signals of more refined qualities deep within other peoples' minds and hearts. People who are more settled inside themselves, who have less inner noise, are naturally more effective listeners.

Prompting other people by giving them both non-verbal and verbal signals helps others be more comfortable in continuing to interact with you. Effective use of questioning directly engages others in giving you more information that supports increased understanding and clarity. Matching some of the words or phrases used by other people demonstrates that you are listening carefully. It directly encourages the communication process by attuning your statements to the thoughts and feelings they are trying to communicate.

Having covered introductory skills that develop more sensitive attention to the process of communication, we now move into the deeper and more important communication skills. The next two sections on listening and emotion management skills represent core skills that you will want to focus on extensively, in order to refine them and apply them with the right timing.

LISTENING SKILLS

Once you have developed effective attending to outer clues and can engage others in communication, the next level of skills involves actively helping people feel comfortable in expressing deeper thoughts and feelings. These skills are sometimes called active listening skills, but the key issue is attentive or careful listening. They involve more careful attentiveness and active participation in the process of listening. But what is more important about the skills is that they support the expression of emotions in order to get to deeper levels of thinking and feeling in communication. These skills are among the most useful to develop. Listening and emotion management skills are the skills to focus on so you can use them at just the right time in your interactions with others.

Listening skills are basic communication tools that are designed to help you listen more carefully and help others express themselves more deeply. These skills may seem a bit artificial at first, but they become more natural and smooth with practice. Highly skilled communicators may not use these skills all the time in a formal way, but they certainly incorporate them at least informally in their communication to show they are listening and to connect more deeply with others.

These also are key skills in therapeutic communication that effective professional counselors use. The chapters in this level of communication skills include summarizing, validating, and empathizing. These three skills basically reflect a sequence of levels of depth of listening. They don't have to be applied in a sequence, but do involve deepening levels of skill in listening.

Much ordinary conversation is just reacting back and forth to the words people are saying to each other. There is little consideration or attention to each other's current emotional state, and whether the information is actually received. An important theme of the book is to become more attentive to the subtler energy flow in the process of communication. These skills foster sensitivity to the timing of the process of communication—when to listen and when to speak—in order to foster deeper, more effective communication.

CHAPTER 13
SUMMARIZING

 Summarizing refers to restating briefly in your own words what other people have just expressed to you, without changing the meaning.

1. It can be frustrating to say something, but then from the person's reply you can't tell if you were understood or even heard. Healthy communication requires listening and demonstrating you have heard what was said to you. The communication skill of summarizing is for this purpose, and it is one of the more important skills. It is putting into your own words in brief form what was said to you. It proves that you listened and understood. When you've shown you listened, people will be more willing to listen to you.

2. For example, let's say you'd like to tell your father you wish he would spend more time with you. You are shy about it, so you start with, 'Do you remember that weekend last year when the dog got lost in the woods and we spent the whole day calling him? I felt so stupid when Rambo-bo-bo-bo echoed down the canyon! That trip was fun. There's nothing to do around here; I hate doing dishes; I want to move to Uncle Ed's.' If your father was not listening carefully, he might think you were just complaining about chores. He might say, 'Those dishes won't clean themselves; get to it.' You wanted to say you had fun with your father, but instead you got criticized for stalling on chores. You may wonder if he cares at all about what you feel.

3. The way to avoid miscommunication like this is to show you listened. The first step is to stop what you are doing, turn to the person talking to you, and pay attention. If something you are doing is important and has priority, then say, 'Please wait a minute and I'll listen right after this.' Right after you finish what you were doing, then actually listen carefully, and demonstrate you listened by repeating back in your own words what was said to you.

4. Returning to the example, if the father listened and summarized, he might say, 'You had fun on the trip last year, you hate doing dishes, and you want to get away and live with Uncle Ed.' When he showed that he heard what you said, you then might be confident to say that what you really want is to spend more time with him. Then he would understand the original point that was hard for you to express.

5. Summarizing helps clarify things by putting them into simpler terms. But it is important to stick to what was said without elaborating or reading things into it that were not in the statement to you. Simply repeat back the basic content of what was said to you, without changing the meaning. Avoid trying to analyze or figure out what the other person really meant. Put the other person's statement into simple words that are directly to the point.

6. Back to the example, if the father didn't listen carefully, he might have misunderstood and said, 'So you hate being forced to do chores and want to move out. Go ahead, I'm tired of your complaining.' Then both of you may get upset and a chance for healthy communication would have deteriorated into hurt feelings. An entire childhood of miscommunication like this can contribute to an unhappy, angry, cynical, and defiant young adulthood.

7. To protect from missing the point in your summarizing, ask if you got it right, such as by saying, 'Is that correct?' or, 'Is this what you were saying?' Then the person can clarify any misunderstanding. It is a great way to get more information. It is also very important for protecting you from reacting too quickly and possibly harshly to what someone just said to you.

8. Here's another example. Let's say one of your employees says, 'I guess I didn't get those instructions right. Is it going to cost me? No one mentioned it after the meeting and I thought this other job had priority. It's hard to hear with that machine right outside your office!' The employee appears to be expressing two things: it's hard to hear in your office; and he is worried about his job. You demonstrate you heard him by summarizing, 'Your saying it's hard to hear instructions in my office, and you want to know if the mistake will affect your job, right?' If correct, then you can deal with each point.

9. Summarizing is not just parroting, mirroring, paraphrasing, or reflecting back the same words. Although repeating what the person said is better than not listening at all, it can sound artificial, and even sarcastic. Attentive listening is required to be able to summarize accurately. It does take practice to do this in a way that sounds natural, but sounding unnatural while you practice is a small price to pay for learning healthy communication. Summarizing is less crucial to use formally once you have learned how to listen. But even then it is quite useful at times to protect against reacting impulsively.

10. Some people who think they are good communicators view the skill of summarizing as a waste of time. Summarizing really means just to listen carefully and then prove that you heard what was said by restating the key points. Unfortunately even so-called good communicators can get into habits of not listening. There are many levels of depth to listening and summarizing. Demonstrating you listened by summarizing goes a long way toward helping people feel more comfortable with you and fostering effective communication.

Examples of How to Use of This Skill

EXAMPLE 1

Ineffective use: Jack says to his wife, Jill, that he is somewhat interested in the house they looked at yesterday, but doesn't want to make a decision for a few days. He wants to think about the effect it will have on being farther away from other family members. Jill tries to summarize, 'You are afraid to commit to the new house, probably because your mother may not like you moving six more miles away.' Jack replies, 'I didn't say that; it is so frustrating when you change the meaning of what I say.'

Effective use: Jill summarizes Jack's comment: 'You want to take a few days to consider the new house. One of the issues is the increased distance from our family. Is this an accurate description of what you are thinking about the house?'

EXAMPLE 2

Ineffective use: Judy explains to her mother that she nearly had an accident on Main and Pine Streets about 8:45 this morning. This red Mazda pulled around a blue truck waiting to turn left just as Judy was turning left to go north on Pine and the truck was turning to go south on Pine. The Mazda slammed on the brakes, stopping a couple feet from her car and nearly sliding sideways into the truck. Her mother tries to restate what Judy said: 'You almost got into an accident with a blue truck and a red car about 8:45 when you were driving in the intersection at Main Street and tried to turn onto Pine Street. The car and truck nearly collided with you when it slammed on the brakes and skidded close to you. Was the stoplight green or were you trying to turn when it was too late to turn?'

Effective use: Judy's mother says, 'It sounds like you had a very close call driving here this morning.' She might also want to ask, 'Are you alright now, honey?'

EXAMPLE 3

Ineffective use: Floor supervisor Kathy explains to Elaine, the new employee, 'If you decide to leave the floor for lunch or whatever, it is important to close the computer terminal, make sure the cash drawer is properly locked, and set it up with Irene in jewelry to watch for customers needing help, but not to be gone between Noon and 1:15.' Elaine replies, 'You want me to be careful and protect things properly.'

Effective use: Not knowing whether Elaine actually heard her, Kathy continues her training with Elaine: 'Yes, good, and there are four points. Do you recall what they are? Just to be sure, I'll jot them down.'

SUMMARY OF CHAPTER 13: Summarizing

1. Summarizing is restating what someone told you.
2. Summarizing requires listening carefully and sincerely.
3. Summarizing demonstrates to other people that you have listened.
4. Summarizing helps people be more open expressing themselves.
5. Briefly restate using your words, but without changing the meaning.
6. Long-term patterns of miscommunication have very negative effects.
7. At the end of summarizing, ask if you got their meaning correct.
8. Summarizing helps people settle down and feel more comfortable.
9. Summarizing takes practice and involves many levels of subtlety.
10. Summarizing protects against reacting too quickly and impulsively.

CHAPTER 14

VALIDATING

 Validating refers to identifying emotions, naming them, and accepting and encouraging their healthy expression.

1. One of the most important communication skills is to recognize and accept peoples' emotions. This skill is called validating, and it is a deeper form of listening than summarizing. It involves identifying the emotions and feelings a person is expressing at the time, and conveying acceptance of the person's right to express them. The skill of validating encourages others to be more trusting and confident of their own thoughts and feelings, and to be more open with you. It demonstrates that you are sincerely interested in relating to them and care enough to listen on more than just the surface level of communication. This builds trust in relationships. It also helps people settle down more quickly so they can get to the point of working through issues and finding solutions to challenging situations.

2. Summarizing is restating the key content of statements another person said. Validating involves identifying and stating another person's emotions. It may involve attending to non-verbal as well as verbal clues to get a sense of what is likely going on in the person's mind and heart.

3. At times people will state very clearly what they are feeling, such as that they are angry, sad, or happy. But at other times, emotions and feelings are so strong that they are overwhelming and confusing, or are subtle and hard to get in touch with clearly. In cases such as these, it may be quite difficult for people to put what they are feeling into words.

4. Identify the emotion you think is being experienced by naming it, and then asking if you are correct. When helping others identify their own emotions, avoid acting like you know automatically what they are feeling inside, even if you are pretty sure. Phrase it as a question or tentative statement so that they can agree or clarify any misperceptions you may have. Avoid trying to convince them you're right about what they are feeling. Remember, we have direct experience only of our own thoughts and feelings. For the most part, we have only indirect information about other peoples' thoughts and feelings.

5. Focus on emotions being expressed at the current moment. As time passes, it is much more difficult to unravel the web of current feelings and past memories. Information from gestures and other behavior that would help identify past feelings are not available in the same way in the present.

6. If you sense a person may be angry, you might say, 'My sense is that you are frustrated now, and may even be angry, is this right?' or, 'You seem angry, correct?' To

a person who may be afraid, you might say, 'I wonder if you felt frightened by it;' or, 'Are you maybe uneasy or anxious about it?'

7. Responses like, 'You shouldn't feel bad;' or, 'Don't be that way;' or, 'You're always upset,' invalidate feelings and are like saying, 'Your feelings are wrong; don't feel what you feel; listen to what I think you should feel.' Healthy, effective communicators avoid telling others what they should or shouldn't feel.

8. Here's another example. A co-worker comes up to you on a break and says, 'I want to get out of this place. Who needs it anyway.' If your response was something like, 'What are you bellyaching about now?,' your friend likely would not feel supported or respected. He may even get angrier and say, 'Get off my back,' and then just walk away. Also, he could start thinking that there really may be something wrong with him. This can feed self-doubt and confusion, when simple validating could have changed the situation into a healthy communication. To validate, you might say, 'Sounds like you're really frustrated with the job right now, correct?' If he agrees, then you can support his expression of frustration such as by saying, 'Are you comfortable talking about it now?' or, 'Yeah, things can get frustrating around here; what's up?'

9. For another example, let's say that 4-year old Billy skins his knee, runs to his mother, and says, 'Mommy, my knee.' She replies, 'Billy, I'm busy talking to Lea; play in the grass, not on the concrete.' Billy wants emotional support and validation, so he continues, 'But Mommy, my knee, and starts crying.' Mom says, 'Now Billy, stop it, you're not mortally wounded; you're not dying; now go have fun!' Billy becomes confused and hurt, has a big crying spell, and everyone gets angry. Years of miscommunication, in which validating is not used, may lead to deeper emotional challenges in Billy. In the same scenario, Mom validates, 'Billy, you skinned your knee, let's take a look, Honey; does it hurt?' Billy says, 'A little Mommy, but what if I play on the grass, it'll be safer.' 'Good plan, Billy!' This time Billy's feelings are acknowledged and validated. He felt respected, and then he settled down, even gaining the confidence to solve things on his own.

10. Validating gives other people the chance to express emotions in an accepting atmosphere. This immediately reduces miscommunication and distress. When a person's emotions are expressed, listened to receptively, and accepted without being blocked by opposition, criticism, or defensiveness, emotions settle down more quickly and things become more comfortable. People feel supported and encouraged. Validating is one of the most important communication skills, and needs to be practiced regularly. It greatly supports healthy, effective communication.

Examples of How to Use This Skill

EXAMPLE 1

Ineffective use: When Robere comes downstairs for breakfast in a hurry to get to work for an important meeting, his wife notices that he seems kind of tense. She says, 'You sure feel uptight today. What's going on?' Robere gets even more uptight, and says that he is in a hurry and goes to the local restaurant to get a quick breakfast.

Effective use: Robere comes down for breakfast with an intense walk and expression on his face. He asks if breakfast is ready, and says that he can't be late for an important meeting. His wife says, 'Yes, it's ready. Am I right that you're feeling anxious, maybe about the meeting? I'd like to hear about it, if you want to talk while you're eating. If not, then that's fine, too.'

EXAMPLE 2

Ineffective use: Judy walks into the kitchen and says: 'Wow, I'm glad to be here! I really had a close call driving over here. A car nearly crashed into me at Main and Pine. I had to stop and catch my breath afterwards.' Judy's mother tries to validate her, 'Oh honey! You must be terrified. I remember last year the same thing happened to me at that same intersection. This wild driver was going too fast...' Her mother goes on and on about her own experience, without listening at all to her daughter.

Effective use: Judy's mother says, 'You had a close call a few minutes ago and still seem frightened, is that right, honey?' She might also say, 'Do you want to talk about it?'

EXAMPLE 3

Ineffective use: Patti angrily runs into Winton's office and says that everyone just ignored her ideas in the meeting, then she starts sobbing and says that she feels unwanted, unappreciated, and maybe she just doesn't belong at this business. Winton says, 'Yeah, I know exactly how you feel. No one hardly shows any courtesy anymore, but just grin and bear it. It's no big deal, and you shouldn't take it so hard, Patti. You'll get more and more depressed. I know what I'm talking about.'

Effective use: Winton responds to Patti's expressions of emotion: 'Sounds like you're irritated and frustrated about the meeting, and may be sad about the way people responded to you, yes? If you want, I'm up for taking a short walk outside and talking about it awhile. I'd like to hear what happened, if you want to talk more about it now.'

SUMMARY OF CHAPTER 14: Validating

1. Validating involves identifying the emotions a person is expressing.
2. Validating is a deeper level of listening than summarizing.
3. At times it is difficult to identify and express emotions in words.
4. People experience directly only their own inner thoughts and feelings.
5. It is easier to focus on identifying current emotions and feelings.
6. Name the feeling you think is being expressed and ask if you're right.
7. Avoid trying to tell other people what emotions they are having.
8. Ineffective validating results in other people doubting themselves.
9. Validating fosters self-confidence and healthy problem solving.
10. Validating quickly leads to deeper heart-to-heart communication.

CHAPTER 15
EMPATHIZING

 Empathizing refers to expressing genuine acceptance, appreciation, and support for what other people are experiencing in their lives at the moment.

1. The communication skill of empathizing involves sort of stepping into the shoes of another person, being with the person's thoughts and feelings in an open, sincere, and supportive way. Whereas validating is focused on identifying and acknowledging emotions, empathizing involves conveying deeper acceptance of the fundamental goodness of the person.

2. The skill of empathizing basically involves receptivity toward and acknowledgement of others. An important part of this is not evaluating at the moment the appropriateness of a person's' behavior, thoughts or feelings but rather just accepting the situation as it is right now. Convey acceptance through patience, interest, and respect, rather than making judgments about behavior or trying to instruct a person on what you think will help. Giving supportive feedback that helps people improve is a good thing to do only at the right time. It needs to be done after people feel accepted and comfortable, and also only when they are able to listen and want to receive it.

3. You can love people as human beings and God's children, even if you don't agree with or condone their behavior. Empathizing is appreciating a person as a human being who is trying to fulfill goals and plans, whether effectively or not, just like you are. It is expressing compassion toward others, relating with an open heart, being fully present with your attention on the person in a patient and accepting manner.

4. Empathizing involves both perceiving accurately others' thoughts and feelings, and communicating understanding and acceptance. It requires listening without drawing conclusions quickly and trying to solve things immediately. If you draw conclusions too quickly, it is likely you won't gain the understanding and convey the acceptance necessary to empathize.

5. Sometimes sympathy and empathy are considered to be the same thing, but they are a little different. Sympathy usually means feeling sorry for others. Empathy shows support for others' attempts to work through challenging situations. Sympathy is more focused on your feelings of sorrow, and empathy is more focused on other peoples' feelings. Both certainly have their value, but empathy is more positive in reinforcing hope. A sympathetic response might be, 'I really feel sorry for what happened.' An empathic response might be, 'It sounds like a lot is happening right now. That can be very tough to deal with.'

6. An important aspect of empathizing is showing consistency between what you say in words and what you project through postures, gestures, facial expressions, and voice tone. This is being congruent, and it is an important part of being genuine. If your words suggest empathy but your tone of voice suggests sarcasm or your gestures suggest lack of interest, then your attempts to empathize won't be effective. You even may be perceived by others as insincere, fake, and lacking in concern. It is necessary to look with interest, speak with respect, and be patient about what others are feeling and thinking. If you express genuine empathy, frequently people will talk about concerns they first were unwilling to discuss. Genuine empathy is healing.

7. Sometimes non-verbal forms of communication can be more effective than words in empathizing. Sitting with someone patiently can have a comforting effect, without using words at all. If you are unsure what to say, just ask if it is okay to sit quietly with the person. Empathy is not in the words, but rather in genuine willingness to be with the person, share time with the person, and relate to the person as someone you care about or at least accept.

8. Empathizing is a time of listening patiently and accepting life at that moment. It is providing a comforting environment in which others can be in touch with their own emotions, thoughts, and feelings, without interference. It doesn't involve trying to help others change, fix things, or work on solutions at the moment. If you try to engage them in problem solving or try to get them to change their feelings when they are not ready, they won't feel supported. Solution building comes later, after emotions have settled down.

9. Empathizing involves avoiding comments such as, 'There's no need to get so upset;' or, 'You shouldn't feel that way;' or, 'I understand your feelings.' These types of statements can result in others feeling unsupported, and even feel that there is something wrong with their own feelings. Such comments can undermine peoples' confidence in their own feelings and in their self-respect, and may increase feelings of frustration toward you.

10. People will usually give subtle signals when they are ready to think about solutions and options, either by asking you what you think needs to be done, or by engaging you in a conversation about something they are considering. Usually this occurs only after their emotions are allowed to be expressed without judgment. If you are not empathizing effectively, frequently people will repeat what they are feeling to get you to listen, their emotions will get more intense, or they will express a desire to be alone.

Examples of How to Use This Skill

EXAMPLE 1

Ineffective use: Yuri is unfamiliar with his new surroundings. He misses his homeland, and also feels angry that everyone is impatient because he doesn't know exactly how to deal with things. As Yuri starts to explain this to Boris, his cousin who invited him to move to the new country and who now calls himself Bo, Boris jumps in and says: 'We both knew it wouldn't be easy, Yuri. But I'm glad you had the brains to come and stop struggling at home. What you need to do is just not worry about it and keep busy looking for a job. You are intelligent and will get used to things soon. Let's go get some food at the restaurant on the corner. Don't worry, I'll buy.'

Effective use: Boris can tell from Yuri's tone of voice that he might be homesick, and even uncertain about whether the move was the right thing. Boris thinks it might be useful to let Yuri talk about it. He also is really interested in learning about Yuri's perspective after his first month in the new country. Boris says, 'You've certainly seen a lot of new things and have gone through a lot lately. I'm interested to hear your thoughts about how it is different here compared to back home, and what you like and don't like. Would you be willing to talk about it with me now?'

EXAMPLE 2

Ineffective use: Oleph listens to his son, Ted, describe how frustrating it is to sit on the bench most of the time during league games. Oleph replies by refocusing the entire conversation not on his son but on his own emotions and experiences. He says, 'You know, that's how it is sometimes. Your experience is so similar to what it was like for me too, especially in basketball, because I did play first string in baseball. But I didn't get along with the baseball coach either, even though I played a lot. You see, the coach seemed to have the idea that I thought I was better than everyone else, so he used to sort of cut me down to size. I remember him even saying to me...etc. and etc.' Ted responds, 'Oh, I remember I'm supposed to call Jamie this afternoon before he leaves for the weekend. I better go do that now, Dad.'

Effective use: When Oleph's son Ted complains about not being chosen to play much, Oleph says, 'That sounds like a frustrating situation. I'd like to hear what's going on in you about it.' He then just listens, and Ted talks for several minutes about challenges dealing with his coach, and even gets into relations with some of the other boys on the team Ted has trouble with that he has never talked about in the past. At the end of the conversation, Ted thanks his father for listening, even though they don't even talk about how to fix things. Oleph offers to talk more about it another time, maybe tomorrow, or whenever Ted wants.

EXAMPLE 3

Ineffective use: The finance vice president says to the marketing vice president, 'It seems like we're having more and more difficulty sorting out expense reports. I need to investigate it carefully, but have not had the time because of being assigned to the merger planning group. That is much more complicated than any of us thought, due to the intellectual property issues involved.' The marketing vice president reacts with no empathy whatsoever, 'Are you implying that my team is not doing things right? Hey, we've been doing the same thing for the past five years. And the sales market is now so competitive that we are struggling just to meet minimal sales projections. Good luck in checking things out, but we're not the problem!'

Effective use: The marketing vice president responds to the finance vice president, 'Sounds like you've got a lot on your plate right now. Is there something we need to go over together? I don't want to take more of your time, but I'm available to discuss any needed changes, when you want. Do you want to say more about how the merger is going?' Later a meeting is set up to work on the expense reports in which they work well together as a team and come up with some good ideas for improvement.

SUMMARY OF CHAPTER 15: Empathizing

1. Empathizing involves acceptance of who people are and what is going on.
2. Empathizing requires patient listening with openness and interest.
3. Empathizing is associated with being compassionate toward other people.
4. Empathy involves not quickly drawing conclusions about people.
5. Empathy and sympathy are different.
6. Consistent non-verbal and verbal behavior increases genuineness.
7. Empathy can be expressed non-verbally.
8. Empathy does not involve trying to problem solve or fix things immediately.
9. Acknowledge and settle down emotions, before trying to problem solve.
10. People give signals when they are ready to engage in problem solving.

Putting It All Together

Attending, Engaging, and Listening Skills

The skills described so far combine into a sequence of outer to inner levels to form an effective system of communication that emphasizes deeper listening. It involves noticing non-verbal and verbal behavior for clues to feelings and thoughts, and then clarifying and confirming them through active and attentive listening. First attend to gestures and facial expressions, then voice and speech styles, and then use engaging skills to get more information. Finally, use listening skills to confirm your understanding and convey acceptance.

Once you have an idea about what other people are thinking and feeling based on non-verbal and verbal information, then ask open and closed questions. Summarize replies to your questions to demonstrate you are listening. Use validating to verify thoughts and feelings, and empathizing to show respect and acceptance.

Although the attending and engaging skills are useful, you may find that summarizing, validating, and empathizing are the skills to use quickly and regularly. They are the core skills that frequently make the difference whether communication is successful.

Attending skills will help you pay attention to the communication process. Engaging skills will help you listen better. Listening skills will help your attentive listening connect more deeply with people, by helping them settle down.

Use of these skills fosters openness to communication in your own heart and mind, as well as in the hearts and minds of others. You will naturally convey respect and acceptance. Then you may not need to apply these skills in a formal manner. However, they are very useful when dealing with strong emotions in others, and they help protect you from reacting too quickly and losing assertive balance.

The skills of summarizing, validating, and empathizing are especially important to learn how to do effectively. Focus your training on developing these skills. These skills help people settle down emotions and get to the deeper level of problem solving or solution building in the mind, toward the even deeper level of fine feelings in the heart that involve more powerful and fulfilling communication and relationships.

EMOTION MANAGEMENT SKILLS

Emotion management skills also are skills you will want to focus on learning and using at the right time, especially in more challenging interactions with others. They help reestablish and maintain assertive balance in order to foster smoother and deeper communication of thoughts and feelings. They help reduce negative emotions and minimize conflict that results from miscommunication. In addition to the listening skills of summarizing, validating, and empathizing, emotion management skills, especially disarming and disengaging, are core skills for effective communication.

These skills are very useful in order to help other people manage their emotions. But also, they are very helpful for you to manage your own emotions. The skills help foster a smooth, balanced, assertive flow of life energy through the levels of heart, mind, and body that is the basis for healthy communication. They expand the effectiveness of listening skills so that communication can deepen while also remaining constructive and healthy for everyone involved.

The chapters in this category of skills include disarming, disengaging, venting, grounding, and resetting. These skills require perhaps the highest level of assertive balance to be able to use effectively. But when you have learned them well enough to apply them when needed, they are great skills to have that significantly improve communication in challenging circumstances. The key to use these skills is good timing to apply them when needed most.

CHAPTER 16
DISARMING

 Disarming refers to managing the flow of energy to dissipate verbal attacks by expressing acceptance or agreement rather than opposing the attack.

1. Negative emotions sometimes get expressed in aggressive behavior such as verbal attacks. If someone verbally attacks you, or even is just a bit controlling or harsh, your immediate reaction can determine whether things quickly settle down or get worse. Disarming is the skill that helps you avoid miscommunication in these circumstances. The key is not to oppose or resist negative emotional energy when expressed toward you or in your presence.

2. It is easy to get defensive in response to offensive aggressiveness, to lose assertive balance, and to attack back quickly. Unfortunately this results in a lose-lose power struggle in which both people can be emotionally harmed. When negative emotions are directed at you, the assertive response is to help the person express them without over-reacting in a defensive manner.

3. When negative energy is directed at you, it is best to get out of the way and not oppose it. At that moment, the person needs to be heard rather than to hear from you. They are outputting, not inputting, and it is not effective to defend yourself or try to correct any misunderstandings right then. The person is not able to receive input, listen, and reason things through at the moment. It is almost as if the ears are not connected to the mind at that moment.

4. Accepting the person's point and agreeing in some manner right in the first few seconds can avoid conflict. Find something you can agree with, and validate it. Make an unqualified agreeing response without hesitation, rebuttal, sarcasm, or attempts to clarify or correct. Avoid use of, 'Yes, but…,' 'However,' 'On the other hand,' 'Wait a minute, you said…,' 'I didn't mean….,' 'That isn't what you said before,' and similar opposing responses. Admit even a very minor mistake, and be flexible enough to apologize. Even if you are completely right and others are wrong, find something with which you can agree. At the moment, it is more effective to be on their side than to defend your pride.

5. Deal with emotions first, then reasons. Emotions are rarely dealt with effectively using logic and reason first, but rather by listening and acceptance first. The issue may have very little to do with the emotions. For example, a person may have built up frustration from a rough day at work, and is now attaching that emotion to some minor issue directed at you. If you don't oppose, and instead help the person express the emotion and settle down, the person is much more likely to realize that the issue wasn't important. He or she may then say sometime like, 'I guess I'm just a little stressed out today.'

6. However, agreeing immediately doesn't mean admitting to something that isn't true. Most often there will be at least some grain of truth in what the person said. It may be that you could have been precisely on time, or you could have been a little more careful or thoughtful. This is the issue to recognize and agree with at the moment. If there is nothing you can agree with, at least respect their point, or at the minimum acknowledge that they have the right to express themselves. After emotions settle down, then you can assert yourself and explain your perspective. Timing is crucial.

7. For example, if a person says, 'Why didn't you get that done?' an effective response is not to give an explanation or excuse, but rather to say, 'You're right; I haven't done it, and I apologize.' After a moment, you might add, 'Do you want to discuss how to deal with it?' Repeating similar phrases can dissipate the other peoples' anger because you showed respect, even if they are being unreasonable. Frequently the person will say something like, 'No big deal, just get it done,' indicating a little empathy and no longer attacking.

8. Another disarming response is to say: 'You seem upset right now, right? Your viewpoint is important, and I want to work this out. Do you want to talk about it now?' Repeat similar steps until things settle down. Another way is to say something like, 'That's a good point; I wasn't looking at it quite that way. I want to think on it, and get back to you after considering it;' or say, 'I respect your point. I want to think about it and talk to you further about it.'

9. The word 'why' frequently signals verbal attack, such as when someone says, 'Why are you late?' 'Why do I have to do it?' 'Why aren't you listening?' 'Why do you care?' 'Why do I care?' You may find that people respond less defensively to expressions such as, 'What are the reasons that...?' or, 'How come...?' or, 'What is your understanding about...?' The words 'never' and 'always' are also used frequently in verbal attacks, and are worth avoiding.

10. Healthy, effective communicators in positions of authority are able to listen to criticism and are self-confident and flexible enough to apologize quickly. They manage the subtle flow of energy in communication, applying disarming just when it is needed most. The person really in charge is the one in charge of his or her own emotions who manages situations to avoid conflict, not the one who 'pulls rank,' threatens, shouts people down, or puts up the most aggressive defense. Being in charge means managing yourself and helping others manage their own emotions, resulting in healthy progress on mutual goals and plans. It rarely means forcing others to comply with you.

Examples of How to Use This Skill

EXAMPLE 1

Ineffective use: Steve says to his wife, 'I told you not to tell anyone about the tax issue yet. Now you'll get us in trouble again. I'm really tired of you making me angry and complicating things. You just never end up listening, do you?' His wife responds, 'I'm sorry. I was watching the shopping channel and wanted to hear the sale price on that bracelet, what did you say? I guess I get distracted a lot, I'm really, really, really sorry, honey, but sometimes the shopping channel does have good buys, especially jewelry. '

Effective use: Steve's wife replies to his criticism: 'Your right, I wasn't listening, and I apologize for being distracted.'

EXAMPLE 2

Ineffective use: Hudson walks into the den where his father is watching TV and says: 'Dad, you know my friend, Spyder, he just got his driver's license and his father bought him an almost new Spider convertible yesterday. I guess he's really pumped about it. Let's talk about the car I want after I complete driver's education. I'm not going to be driving the mini-van!' Hudson's father replies: 'Now calm down. We'll talk, but can't you see I'm into the Hawkeye game at the minute? Later, bud.'

Effective use: Hudson's father replies, 'You're right, Spyder is probably excited about his new car, and also you're right that we need to talk about what to do when you get your license. Can we decide on a time to talk now, or is it better to talk when your driver's education classes start next year?'

EXAMPLE 3

Ineffective use: Shannon comes in from school, drops her coat and books on the carpet, and turns on the TV. Mom comes in and says: 'Shannon, please pick up your things and take them to your room.' Shannon replies, 'As soon as I walk in, you always yell at me. Do you just wait for me to get home so you have someone to criticize?' Mom says, 'I'm not trying to make you mad. You're a very capable and smart girl; you can help a little.' Shannon says, 'What's the big deal? I don't leave stuff there all the time.' Mom says, 'Well, honey, I've put your coat away every day this week.' Shannon shouts, 'You have not! I didn't wear it Monday. It was warm out, duh!'

Effective use: Mom says, 'Hi, honey, things OK?' Shannon snaps back, 'Could you just not ask any questions? I'm tired, I don't want to talk, I just want to be alone for a while.' Mom replies, 'Sure, I can do that.' A minute later, Shannon says, 'Kim ignored me again. She's so rude.' Mom listens to Shannon a couple minutes and she settles down. Then Shannon says, 'Oh, Mom, I have to tell you what Mr. Zimmerman did in class today. It was so funny!' Mom says, 'I'll feed Princess, can you put your coat and books in your room, and then I want to hear about Mr. Zimmerman, OK?' Shannon says, 'Oh, all right.' They quickly do the chores and then sit together to talk. Shannon tells a very funny story about Mr. Zimmerman, the history teacher.

SUMMARY OF CHAPTER 16: Disarming

1. The key to disarming is not to oppose the other person.
2. Help others express emotions, rather than trying to defend yourself.
3. A verbally attacking person needs to express emotions right then.
4. Accepting the person's point right away can avoid conflict.
5. Deal first with settling down emotions, and then the reasons or issues.
6. Find some point to accept or agree with at the start.
7. Agreeing helps get the person on your side to cooperate with you.
8. Postpone stating your perspective until others can actually listen to you.
9. Why, always, and never can signal verbal attack and are helpful to avoid.
10. Healthy communicators manage the flow of energy to avoid conflict.

CHAPTER 17
DISENGAGING

 Disengaging refers to managing the timing of communication in order to maintain balance and avoid harmful miscommunication.

1. The basic skills described so far will help you deal effectively with the levels of behavior, mind, and heart in yourself and other people in most situations. But on rare occasion, things may become so challenging that something more is needed. The communication skill of disengaging is very helpful in these more challenging situations.

2. Disengaging includes managing your own emotional involvement, or backing off physically, or leaving the situation for a while. Effective disengaging does these in a manner that builds more trust in relationships.

3. People can't 'make you' mad, sad, or glad. For the most part, no one can force you to have a particular emotion. Emotions are produced inside our hearts, minds, and bodies—not from outside. Healthy communicators recognize this and take full responsibility for their own emotions. We choose our own reactions. We may choose to build a habit of angry reactions to negative comments, but we don't have to react that way, and others don't make us respond that way. We can train ourselves to give healthy, balanced responses, in the same way any positive habit is learned. It is important to recognize this, and to avoid comments that foster feelings of powerlessness, such as asking, 'How did that *make* you feel?'

4. If negative energy is directed toward you, it helps to remember that it is the other person's emotions, not yours. The negative emotions have very little to do with you. You might have contributed to them, but you did not cause them. Disengaging by not taking it personally helps you work with the person's emotions, rather than getting off balance yourself. People may try to get you emotionally upset, but it will only contribute to more challenges. Consider yelling and name-calling as calls for you to help others dissipate negative energy and regain balance. Use your mind to apply communication skills in order to avoid negativity from going deep into your own heart and disrupting your own feeling level.

5. Sometimes a simple statement such as, 'I'm starting to feel uncomfortable,' can help the person recognize what is happening with your emotions. The person likely doesn't really want you to get upset, but may be too caught up in the emotions to notice. This provides an external gauge for the person to help understand what's going on in the environment—especially in you.

6. Disengaging may also involve physically backing off and giving the person space and time to settle down. Being quiet and not trying to communicate sometimes

can help. Speaking calmly and standing to the side rather than directly in front also may help people become less angry or defensive.

7. If it has to be taken further, the next step may be to take a time-out. You might say, 'I need to go settle down. I don't want to say anything hurtful. I'll be back in 20 minutes.' It is appropriate to remove yourself from the situation to stay out of harm's way and prevent more distress that could damage body, mind, and heart. As another example, you might tell the person, 'I feel confused about how to communicate right now. I need to go settle down a few minutes. Can we talk again in a half hour?' If you do this, however, be sure to try again no more than 30 minutes later. Time-outs need to be followed up with time-ins. Accept responsibility for your own emotions, and don't blame the other person for you needing a time-out. But if you're okay and are remaining assertively balanced, then stay with it and use your skill to help the other person settle down.

8. With someone you communicate with regularly, such as a loved one, agree in advance on a time-out procedure both of you can follow. Include a specific length of time, physical separation such as going on a walk outside, and re-engaging at the end of the agreed-upon time period. In close relationships, a minimum of 30-60 minutes of time-out is needed. A helpful time-out format allows either partner to call for a time-out. The person who calls for the time-out decides how long of a time-out, and the other decides who will leave during the time-out. The partner who called time-out has the responsibility to re-engage at the end of the time-out. Disengaging requires re-engaging, in order to build trust.

9. Another form of time-out involves agreeing not to talk about a specific issue for a period of time. This limited time-out might last at least half a day, and possibly weeks or more. It might be that the agreement is to avoid talking about a particular issue until after some other specific event has taken place. At times it is worthwhile to take an extended time-out from dealing with a difficult issue, within yourself as well as between you and another person. An emotional vacation of postponing a highly charged issue for even weeks can promote a more productive perspective when the issue is revisited.

10. Help others gain balance only when you're in balance. As soon as you are significantly challenged, it is better not to stay in the situation. It is important not to risk giving others control over your own emotions. Losing balance and becoming negative decreases your effectiveness. Avoid letting out your own emotions when others haven't agreed to help you do this. Leave and settle down, either on your own or with the skilled support of a third person. Then re-engage when you are settled enough to communicate effectively.

Examples of How to Use This Skill

EXAMPLE 1

Ineffective use: Neal is staying late at the office, meeting and getting acquainted with new staff. He knows Karen, his wife, is upset about it. They go to dinner, and when she brings it up, he says, 'Let's not spoil a nice evening out, honey. Can we talk about it later?' Karen says nothing. Neal is happy to avoid the talk, and hopes she'll forget to bring it up later so he won't have to deal with it at all.

Effective use: While eating dinner at a restaurant with her husband, Karen says, 'Honey, it seems like you've been late at the office a lot lately. Your daughter and I both need to spend time with you regularly.' Neal responds, 'Honey, let's not talk about it at dinner, it's just that things are busy right now.' Karen says, 'You never want to talk about anything; I'm getting really annoyed.' Neal says, 'Can't you see I'm trying to make a living for us?' Karen then realizes things could get difficult, and she remembers to validate and disengage. She says, 'I'm about to say something I don't mean, so you're right, this isn't the time to talk about it. I'd like to go for a walk to settle down. I need a little break for a few minutes.' Neal says, 'If you need to, we can discuss it now.' Karen says, 'I feel too sensitive right now.' Neal says, 'OK, I guess we need to set up a time. How about Sunday after lunch?' Karen replies, 'Fine; I'll be back in 10 minutes.'

EXAMPLE 2

Ineffective use: When his wife mentioned that there's not enough money in the checkbook to pay the credit card bill this month, Larry tries to explain that sales have been slower the last three months. When she points out that they've barely been getting by for two years now, they haven't gone on a cruise or vacation for two years, and they still have the car they bought three years ago, Larry responds, 'I'm out of here. You're just making me upset, and nothing gets solved. I'll be back later, and maybe you will be able to talk rationally about this then.'

Effective use: In response to his wife's comments, Larry says, 'I want to talk this through with you, and I need to settle down first to hear what you have to say without over-reacting. Can we plan a time to go into it carefully, and give me a chance to calm down first? How about after lunch we walk to the lake and have a pow-wow?'

EXAMPLE 3

Ineffective use: Maria's partner, Corinna, chastises Maria as soon as she walks into the shop. She says, 'You left the window open in the office again. Maria, this has to stop. We are going to get robbed if the shop is not locked up properly. How many times do I have to tell you? It's ridiculous, Maria, it's just stupid!' Maria responds, 'I'm not stupid, Corinna, and you make plenty of mistakes too, you know, like leaving the cash drawer open a lot, and leaving the flower pots outside the door.' Corinna responds, 'That's stupid, Maria, I didn't call you stupid, don't put words in my mouth.' Maria says, 'We're both stupid for yelling like this. Why don't you go somewhere for the morning and I'll stay here and nail all the windows shut!'

Effective use: When Corinna starts yelling, Maria responds, 'You're right, Corinna, the shop must be locked up properly each night.' This immediately settles things down a bit, and Corinna says that she didn't mean to be so harsh, but she is concerned about it. Corinna says, 'What can we do to make it better?' Then Maria asserts herself and says: 'You may have forgotten that I was gone all day yesterday to pick up the silk flowers in Riverside, and James watched the shop.' But then Maria starts to get upset, and says: 'Why do you always blame me for everything that goes wrong?' Corinna replies, 'You hired James, didn't you?' Maria says, 'Yes, so what, and I took you in as partner, but not so you could yell and complain all the time!' Corinna finally realizes she is not achieving anything constructive and is about to lose it big time. She says, 'I'm about to lose it here, and don't want to harm our friendship. I spoke too soon and I'm sorry. I need to be alone a while to settle down. Do you want to do the bank and post office errands, or should I? It seems like we need to have a business meeting and work on things, including security procedures. When can we talk about it?'

SUMMARY OF CHAPTER 17: Disengaging

1. Disengaging helps in very challenging emotional situations.
2. Disengaging can involve backing off emotionally or physically.
3. Consider negative emotions as calls for assistance in communicating.
4. No one can 'make you mad' or 'make you happy.'
5. Back off physically to give space and time for people to settle down.
6. It is appropriate to express discomfort and get out of danger.
7. Time-outs are important for managing emotions and communication.
8. Agreed upon time-outs require re-engaging at the end of the time-out.
9. A time-out might involve agreeing not to talk about a specific issue.
10. Engage with another person only when you can remain balanced.

CHAPTER 18

VENTING

 Venting refers to managing the expression of strong emotions such as aggressive anger in order to avoid destructive miscommunication.

1. When people find it difficult to communicate with assertive balance due to strong emotions such as fear or anger, they sometimes hold them in and don't express them. This non-assertive style of behavior can be a helpful temporary strategy that is less damaging than reacting harshly or aggressively. Taking time to settle down, instead of reacting impulsively, can reestablish balance. But if unexpressed emotions build up, the skill of venting can be helpful.

2. The term venting is related to airing out or providing ventilation to avoid fumes or pressure building up to the exploding point. As a communication skill, venting involves expressing feelings and thoughts freely in a safe, protected environment. Miscommunication commonly results from trying to express goals and plans when emotions are not settled, either in the person expressing the thoughts and feelings or in the person who at the time can't listen without getting overinvolved. Venting can release some of the build-up of emotional energy that otherwise might be held in or explode out. But it doesn't mean just complaining or yelling any time and place you feel.

3. Venting is a special communication skill requiring a safe environment to express strong emotions that will not result in negative effects. Going on long walks and thinking things through, distracting yourself with engaging activities such as a funny movie, and vigorous physical exercise such as chopping wood or playing sports can help settle down strong negative emotions. It also helps to express the emotions directly, either by writing them out, called journaling, or talking them out with a supportive helper, a third person not directly involved who listens without trying to fix things.

4. The supportive helper needs to know how to help someone vent emotions. Helpers need to apply effectively the communication skills of listening, questioning, disarming, summarizing, and especially validating. They need to be able to maintain privacy and confidentiality. The helper role doesn't involve trying to fix the problem, getting emotionally involved, or taking personally the potentially less refined or harsher speech of a person who is venting emotions. If someone is angry for no apparent reason, they may be using you to help vent emotions, without letting you know that the emotions aren't about you. Recognizing this helps avoid taking it personally.

5. It is important that the emotions expressed while venting are not taken personally and are not thought about or dwelt upon afterward. It is simply an opportunity

to blow off a little pressure so that subsequent communication is more effective, but under safe conditions. Strong or critical words expressed are to be forgotten by both the person venting and the helper. The helper provides a safe environment with no negative consequences. Venting helps manage emotions for more assertive balance at a later time when the original issue is addressed directly with the people who are involved.

6. In close-knit extended families more common in prior generations, venting was one helpful role filled by family elders. An elder listened in private as a family member thought out-loud about a concern. Occasionally the elder offered a bit of wisdom through an appropriate story that fostered deeper reflection, but avoided forcing a particular view or a resolution to the issue. Today this level of communication skill is rare.

7. Venting also provides an opportunity to practice being assertive, in preparation for communicating in a smoother way that is easier for other people to listen and understand. It relieves some of the frustration from not being assertively balanced when the initial situation came up. It also can help clarify feelings and thoughts, as well as clarify how to express them better when the issues are dealt with directly.

8. For example, let's say your supervisor was critical of you in public. You had the impulse to tell him off, but knew it could become worse. You chose not to reply then, but did feel resentful. At home, you told your wife what happened and she let you blow off steam by venting about how your supervisor had no right to attack you. While venting, you remembered the supervisor just returned to work after surgery. The next week the supervisor seemed less tense, so you asserted yourself by requesting that feedback be given in private. The supervisor listened, gave a slight apology, and you both felt respected. Nothing further was needed—except thanking your spouse.

9. Venting can involve natural shifts back and forth from anger to feeling down, from mad to sad, from blaming others to blaming oneself, from aggressiveness to non-assertiveness. If a person expresses only sadness or only anger, don't try to get them to express the other emotion. As appropriate, suggest talking with a counselor to learn emotion management.

10. Venting is not necessary for healthy communication. It doesn't solve anything by itself. But it can help regain balance in preparation for healthy assertive communication when you later re-engage with the person to work further on the initially challenging issue.

Examples of How to Use This Skill

EXAMPLE 1

Ineffective use: Karen expressed anger to her husband, Neal, for staying late at the office. She also complains about it to her mother. Her mother is not a skilled communicator and feeds the anger with old doubts about her daughter's choice for a marriage partner. Neal is annoyed that Karen is pushing the issue, but also feels a little guilty about his fascination with an attractive new staff-member in marketing. Neal tries to get support from his secretary by asking her if it's reasonable for his wife to be upset about him working extra to pay for the new house, trying to get his secretary emotionally involved in supporting him.

Effective use: Karen calls her best friend, Nancy, and says she needs to talk. On a long walk, Nancy lets Karen express her anger toward Neal. After a while, Karen settles down and says she knows how to bring up her feelings to Neal this weekend and is confident they will come to a workable schedule. Neal's brother stops by the office to take him to lunch. When his brother asks how things are going with the family, Neal says fine and changes the topic, but eventually brings up his fascination with the new staff member and admits to some of his feelings. His brother just listens and lets Neal think it through himself, finally getting to the point of saying he realizes he hasn't been home much in the evenings. When Karen and Neal talk, they end up scheduling regular family nights with everyone home together.

EXAMPLE 2

Ineffective use: Rudolfo decides he should go to the flower shop to pick up something for his wife, after they have a major argument about problems with their four teenagers. He has to wait while the shopkeeper continues on the phone, complaining to her mother about her partner's irresponsibility. Noticing his growing impatience, the shopkeeper interrupts the phone call and says, 'Is there something you need?' He replies, 'Well, I need assistance, I'm a customer, at the moment anyway.' The shopkeeper says to her mother that she has to go and will call again later, then hangs up, turns to him and says, 'Yes, what do you want?' Rudolfo says, 'You know, you women are all alike. You talk and talk to each other, but don't deal with the real issues in front of you. I just don't know how to make this point clear. It's like dealing with another teenager, and I already have four at home that are always on the phone, never doing anything practical around the house. You're a female, how does someone get through to you on a matter like this?' The shopkeeper replies, 'If you have four teenagers, you don't have a clue about what your wife goes through every single day.'

Effective use: Rudolfo calls his uncle and invites him to lunch, saying he needs to talk about several things that are building up in him. He does this every couple months, and the uncle is a good person to let him talk, without spreading rumors. He decides to stop by the bookstore and get a book on parenting of teenagers that he can read and discuss with his wife. Afterwards, Rudolfo stops by the flower shop for some flowers to put on the table for Sunday dinner, which he knows his wife will appreciate. When the shopkeeper is on the phone and is somewhat rude to him, he lets it go, but does explicitly say that he appreciates being given attention. He also plans to explore other flower shops in the area.

EXAMPLE 3

Ineffective use: Frustrated about the way the board chairperson is putting her off about getting a new computer for the program she directs, Helen calls another board member and expresses her opinions about the situation. The following week Helen overhears the chairperson comment to other staff about how some people complain behind other peoples' backs and think that everything has to be done immediately on their own schedule.

Effective use: Helen recognizes she is getting quite frustrated about not having a computer to keep track of the many areas of the program she directs. She calls her mother, who has lots of business experience and has been a good support in the past. She knows her mother will listen, not criticize or try to tell her what to do immediately, and won't blab to anyone on the board of directors. After blowing off some steam, Helen comes up with a good plan on her own that she wants to try out.

SUMMARY OF CHAPTER 18: Venting

1. Strong unexpressed feelings sometimes build up inside.
2. Venting involves expressing strong emotions in a safe setting.
3. Venting requires a safe and supportive environment.
4. Venting can help relieve pressure and maintain balance.
5. A supportive helper needs to have excellent communication skills.
6. Emotions expressed while venting are not dwelled on later.
7. Elders used to provide the service of venting within extended families.
8. Venting helps prepare people for assertive problem solving.
9. Venting provides helpful practice that clarifies thoughts and feelings.
10. Venting is useful, but not a necessary part of healthy communication.

CHAPTER 19
GROUNDING

 Grounding refers to resting, then attending to body, mind, and heart in order to re-establish assertive balance and a smoother flow of life energy.

1. At times the mind-body system can get off balance and the flow of life energy through heart, mind, body and behavior can become either sluggish or choppy. Communication can then become non-assertively protective or aggressively defensive, even when the goal was balanced assertiveness. This is usually due to getting tired or straining, frequently from dealing with other non-assertive or aggressive people. The body's inner intelligence gives signals such as aches or pains to let us know that things are out of balance. The communication skill of grounding helps to tune in to these signals and attend to heart, mind, and body in order to take a little better care of ourselves and smooth out the natural flow of energy through us.

2. Grounding is associated with getting your feet back on the ground when balance is lost. Sometimes not being grounded refers to being too much in your head, meaning overinvolved with thinking and not well-connected with body, emotions, and feelings. This is related to intellectualizing, or analyzing ideas too much while ignoring emotions and feelings. But it can also relate to being too much in your heart, meaning overinvolved with emotions and not well-connected with mind and clear thinking. This involves dwelling too much on emotions and not keeping in touch with rational thinking and solution building, sometimes called emotionalizing. Balanced assertiveness is healthy and effective, rather than intellectualizing or emotionalizing.

3. The communication skill of grounding involves taking a little time to attend to the signals coming from the body, mind, and heart, and also taking simple steps to reduce stress and inner noise to help reestablish balance. It involves relaxing and settling down to increase mind-body coordination to function more smoothly. Grounding can be very helpful during time-outs in the skill of disengaging, in order to help settle down and get to the place where you can effectively work on solutions.

4. Basically the key means of grounding is to rest. Most anything that naturally promotes deep rest is useful for grounding. For the most part, the deeper the rest, the more grounded. If strong emotions have built up inside due to a non-assertive pattern, sometimes a little venting also can help so it is easier to settle down and recognize the need to rest. The poor judgment that sneaks in to complicate daily life due to fatigue is hard to recognize. When you get bogged down, or when people seem to be holding you back or getting in the way, these may signal that grounding rest is needed.

5. One simple approach that helps provide a little grounding right away is deep breathing. Take three or four deep breaths by expanding both the diaphragm and the chest. This is the type of breathing singers use to relax and energize their voices.

6. Another quick grounding exercise is self-massage. One simple method is to massage each finger and palm, and also the scalp including ears and neck. This can both relax and wake you up a little. A warm bath, then lying down afterwards, also can have a comfortable, relaxing, and grounding effect.

7. Simple stretching exercises and muscle relaxation methods such as progressive relaxation that take only a few minutes also can settle things down. Tightening muscles and then relaxing them, such as hands, arms, legs, and feet while sitting quietly, and then relaxing for a minute or so with your eyes closed, is useful for creating at least some immediate grounding.

8. Physical exercise also is very useful for grounding. For example, taking a short walk and attending in turn to each of the senses-- hearing, touch, sight, taste, and smell—is enjoyable and enlivening. Sports such as golf and swimming can have a positive grounding influence as long as you don't get emotionally unbalanced with concern over the score. In general, activities that use different skills than used in work have grounding effects. This is sometimes called cross training. For example, walking, biking, golf, and swimming are good cross-training activities for a desk job; team sports are good if you work by yourself; solitary activities are good for jobs with lots of interaction with people. Quiet activities help balance intense, hectic work.

9. Scientifically-validated stress management techniques, especially effortless meditation, are the most effective for rest and rejuvenation. A profound form of grounding, direct inner experience of the ground of Being, is discussed in the chapter on the communication skill of unifying at the end of this book. Also, medical science is beginning to confirm that certain forms of natural therapy based on music, touch, colors, herbs, teas, and aromas have a healthy, soothing influence. Some of these come from ancient approaches to natural medicine known for centuries to be enjoyable and gentle ways to create balance in mind-body functioning and help prevent disease.

10. After things settle down, it can be helpful to review goals and plans. First settle down, and then strengthen the flow of energy through heart, mind, and behavior by clarifying your goals and plans. A simple way to remember this is to ask yourself, 'What is my GPA (Goal, Plan, Action)?'

Examples of How to Use This Skill

EXAMPLE 1

Ineffective use: Sean is enjoying so much his computer job that he is working most all the time, including late into the evenings. He realizes he needs to take breaks periodically, so he finds it convenient to watch DVD movies on his computer. He also has fun chatting with people from around the world and playing games with them on the Internet. However, he feels so distant from his family and old friends that he just doesn't enjoy doing things with them anymore. He has noticed more frequent headaches and lower energy, but these seem to go away after sleeping a while.

Effective use: Sean realizes that he needs to offset the stress of working on the computer so much. He now makes a point of getting outside 10 minutes every couple hours. He goes on short walks, and has lunch outside on the patio. He also has been having dinner with his brother or sisters at least one night each week, and has joined two clubs, one for softball and the other that builds houses for people in need. He has noticed he has more energy and clarity of mind, and he is even considering taking a sailing trip in the Mediterranean.

EXAMPLE 2

Ineffective use: Elka sees that her husband is so busy and absorbed at his work that he is gone from home most of the time, even out of town about half of every week including weekends. She also finds it hard to be with him when he is home, because he's on the cell phone a lot, is restless, and is always busy with little things. She feels it is also making her uptight. She decides to get into yoga and also jogging. She finds from these changes that she has more energy. Now she also is rarely at home, going to yoga class three days a week for three hours, is up to 8 miles of jogging each day, and is working toward running two marathons next month.

Effective use: Frank finds that there is so much pressure in his insurance sales work that it absorbs all of his emotional energy. He also has noticed that he gets angry at people who are slow in their decisions and can't understand the obvious value of his financial recommendations. When his mother calls and points out that this is the first time in three months he has talked to her, he recognizes he is increasingly isolated from family and friends. He makes an agreement with his mother to either call her or visit his parents each week. He finds that he actually enjoys bringing them some Chinese take-out food and just chatting with them regularly. He also decides to have breakfast at the café on the road to his office, where a group of retired guys go each morning to discuss the world situation and to tease each other. He has oatmeal that morning, which seemed to help his digestion, and for the first time in a while laughed quite a bit over the playful teasing the retired men do to each other.

EXAMPLE 3

Ineffective use: When the doctor tells Phil he needs to exercise more and lose weight, he decides to call a meeting at 1:00 PM three days a week in his office. While his staff sits with him and talks about work, he sits on a stationary bike and does some pedaling for exercise. Phil thinks this is a very efficient way to fit exercise into his routine.

Effective use: Phil's doctor tells him that his hypertension is getting worse and that he is at risk of a severe heart attack, or at least costly heart surgery. The doctor recommends exploring natural means to reduce his stress level. He recommends learning how to meditate, because it has been shown through scientific research to be an effective natural means to reduce hypertension and other stress-related health problems. The doctor explained that it may cost some money, but it is a lot cheaper than the time, money, and distress of heart problems. Phil decides to check it out.

SUMMARY OF CHAPTER 19: Grounding

1. The body's inner intelligence signals the need for grounding and rest.
2. Over-involvement in actions, emotions, and thoughts causes ungrounding.
3. Grounding involves taking time to attend to body, mind, and heart.
4. The basic means for grounding is to rest.
5. Deep breathing is a simple, quick grounding technique.
6. Self-massage also can be helpful for grounding.
7. Scientifically-validated, effortless meditation is excellent for grounding.
8. Well-designed exercise and cross-training programs are also useful.
9. Many natural medicine approaches offer helpful grounding methods.
10. After resting, remind yourself of your GPA (Goal, Plan, Action).

CHAPTER 20
RESETTING

 Resetting refers to managing negative emotional reactions by quickly interrupting their development and reestablishing more clarity about goals and plans.

1. The natural direction of life is toward achievement of goals for higher fulfillment. However, sometimes obstacles seem so large that we can't see our way through or around them. The immediate reaction may be to get frustrated or deflated, when in fact a simple change in the situation could free up our energies so that negative emotions don't fully develop.

2. When energy is being expressed in aggressive behavior, it can be difficult to stop. Disarming, disengaging, venting, and grounding are useful skills for averting or reducing the harmful effects of aggressive behavior. Resetting is a related emotion management skill that relies a little more on the connection between thinking and emotion. It involves catching the negative emotion in the process of being expressed from heart and mind into emotional behavior, and interrupting it by delaying it or re-evaluating the situation. The mind structures emotions and other behavior, and can be used to restructure and manage them more effectively.

3. The key to the communication skill of resetting is to delay briefly, or go beyond, the emerging emotional reaction. This can allow time for taking a new perspective that will provide an opportunity for a different approach to emerge, or for the situation to change, or for the emotion to pass on its own. Angry reactions are usually very brief, lasting only a few seconds, unless fueled by more miscommunication or negative ruminating about the issue.

4. Resetting involves building a positive habit of giving yourself a cue to do something that interrupts the negative emotion as soon as signals appear that negative emotions are rising up inside you. These signals might include tightening of muscles in the body such as shoulders, neck, chest, or stomach, standing up rigidly, breathing heavier, frowning or tightening the jaw or lips, talking louder, making stronger hand or arm movements, crossing arms over the chest and other defensive postures, or turning away to hide emotions.

5. One type of resetting is to perform a simple behavior such as taking a deep breath, stretching, pulling off your glasses and rubbing your eyes, laughing a little, or glancing out the window or at something pleasing such as a special photo or painting. This can provide a pause in the sequence of events that reduces the intensity of the moment, which might be enough to take the edge off of the emotions starting to arise.

6. Another useful habit is asking people to clarify what they just said, or repeating back what you think they said, discussed earlier as the skill of summarizing. Anything that pulls attention away from the immediate situation and delays emotional expression a little bit can be helpful.

7. It also can be helpful to get into the habit of asking yourself a question as soon as you notice a negative emotion is coming up, such as, 'Is this really what I want to do?' 'Will what I'm about to say help?' 'Is this a good way to assert myself?' 'Do I want to get upset about this?' 'Do I have to deal with this now?' 'Must I dignify this with a reply?' 'Is it important?' 'Is this a balanced response?' 'What's my opportunity for progress here?'

8. In addition, a standard phrase you can say quickly to yourself can help maintain balance. Here are some examples: 'It's not worth getting into an argument;' 'This isn't how I want to react;' 'I'm stronger than this;' 'This is not consistent with my goals;' 'I know how to handle this well;' 'When in these situations, look for the humor;' 'In the long run, it'll work out okay.'

9. Aggression and other negative reactions generally are due to inadequate planning. Planning includes training in how to deal with situations in which it feels like your buttons get pushed. These buttons are not pushed from outside, but from inside. It is a misunderstanding to think other people can push your buttons. It's a negative habit of giving control of your emotions to others, which needs to be replaced by more positive self-control. With more inner silence and practice of the skill of resetting, you can act with sufficient balance to have a better chance of positive, constructive action. The general approach is to get clearer about your goals, plan specific behaviors consistent with the goals, gently remind yourself of them regularly, and thereby build a habit of reevaluating behavior in terms of your goals as soon as you notice potential conflict may be starting.

10. A more advanced form of resetting is to take your attention entirely out of the immediate situation, using your mind to go beyond the emotions and completely change their direction. This involves taking a moment of inner silence. It is quickly settling down to an expanded mental state that is beyond the developing negative emotional trap. Briefly closing your eyes and resting a moment will sometimes be enough to create this state. This occurs more naturally and spontaneously as inner silence grows. But this certainly doesn't mean forcing yourself to suppress or disregard the emotion and never deal with it.

Examples of How to Use This Skill

EXAMPLE 1

Ineffective use: Samantha was told many times that children should be seen but not heard, so she has made a point of telling herself to keep quiet around her elders, asking herself in these situations, 'What do I have useful to say?' She feels that this protects her from talking unnecessarily. Samantha is shy around adults in general, but does find it easier to be around children.

Effective use: Kelly Ann is getting out of a pattern of taking it personally and reacting defensively when someone is dissatisfied with the clothes she sells in her dress shop. As soon as someone complains, she now courteously asks the person to wait just a minute while she goes into the back and looks up the sales record. This gives her a minute to settle down and not react too quickly. When looking at the record, she also reads a quote in the back office that says, 'A happy customer is a repeat customer.' By doing this, she finds that she doesn't react so defensively, and is able to work with the customer to sort things out constructively. For the first time, recently three customers sent her notes of appreciation for the quality of her services.

EXAMPLE 2

Ineffective use: Dillon recognizes that he is defensive and quick to react when he thinks someone is going to criticize him. He concludes that the only way to deal with it is to force himself not to say anything at all when these situations arise. He does well for a week, but then blows up at his wife and criticizes her in a harsh way that he never intended or wanted to do.

Effective use: Recognizing he is quick to react defensively to other peoples' comments to him that may be even a little bit critical, Dillon makes a point of writing down these instances for two weeks. He finds that they don't happen as much as he had thought, but his response is rarely constructive when it does happen. He devises a plan about how to delay his immediate reaction. He tries out having a standard question to ask, or taking off his glasses and wiping his brow. He finds that removing the glasses is easier to remember, so he tries it out for a month, and finds it is helping and he is getting better at it. It hasn't eliminated all the defensive reactions, but he can see that helps a little. He feels encouraged that applying other skills will help further.

EXAMPLE 3

Ineffective use: Greg asks around his office and finds that quite a few co-workers feel uncomfortable about how he seems to deal with them when he gets uptight and touchy. He thinks he might not be the person for this type of job, because he has to work in close proximity to others a lot. He decides he will look for a job in a smaller office, or maybe even a different type of work where he doesn't have to interact with others much.

Effective use: Greg asks several of his co-workers what they notice about his angry responses to people. The feedback indicates that he seems to get more testy when he and other people are getting tired in the late afternoon. Greg decides to try setting his digital watch to click each hour from three until he finishes work at five. He then takes one minute to close his eyes and relax, sometimes even massaging his eyes gently. It doesn't solve things entirely, but it seems to help enough that he decides to try out other resetting approaches, including putting new landscape pictures in his office cubicle, and to go on a short walk at four o'clock each workday.

SUMMARY OF CHAPTER 20: Resetting

1. A simple change can free us up from rising negative emotions.
2. The mind structures emotions, and can restructure them.
3. Angry emotions usually last only a few seconds.
4. There are many body signals of the onset of negative emotions.
5. Taking a deep breath or stretching can slow emotional expression.
6. Questioning and summarizing can delay the expression of emotions.
7. Asking yourself a question gives time to reevaluate your impulse to act.
8. Standard phrases reminding yourself of plans and goals help resetting.
9. Resetting involves rethinking behavior in terms of your goals.
10. Moments of inner silence help go beyond negative emotional reactions.

Putting It All Together:
Attending, Engaging, Listening, and Emotion Management Skills

Emotion management skills basically are for the purpose of helping maintain balanced assertiveness. They are useful skills to add to attending, engaging, and listening in order to help smooth out the flow of energy through heart, mind, body, and behavior. These skills fit into the sequence of working with the outer levels of body language and emotional behavior to settle things down in order to progress toward deeper inner levels of thinking and feeling in the mind and heart.

Careful attention is fostered by attending to body language, voice quality, and speech style. Attentive listening is fostered by engaging skills that effectively support continuing the process of communication into deeper levels of interaction. Increased receptivity, depth of listening, and openness to deeper communication are fostered by listening skills. Emotion management skills help reestablish and maintain assertive balance in order to deepen communication and avoid miscommunication.

As body and emotions settle down and smooth communication is maintained, the communication process naturally proceeds to the deeper level of mind and thinking. This level is the platform on which healthy teamwork and constructive problem solving—or solution building—can take place. It relates to the next deeper level of communication skills.

SECTION THREE

COMMUNICATION SKILLS ON THE LEVEL OF MIND AND THINKING

This third section of the book primarily deals with the inner level of mind and thinking. This level relates to unobservable, inner thoughts that are expressed in speech and other behavior. The inner level of thinking is a more expressed level than the underlying inner level of feeling. It is focused on the processes of thinking through plans that direct behavior, and of evaluating the results of implementing the plans in behavior.

Once emotions have settled down by use of listening and emotion management skills, then the next deeper level of communication is the level of mind and thinking. This is the level at which effective decision making and solution building take place that are necessary to guide healthy behavior. Communication skills on the level of mind and thinking involve healthy ways of thinking that plan, direct, and implement communication behavior.

The deeper level of feelings in the heart guides the level of thinking in the mind. But the rational thinking mind guides and directs the more expressed level of the body and behavior. The level of the mind collects information from the inner level of heart, and also from the outer level of the environment, and then decides and directs action to fulfill one's own goals and plans while respecting the goals and plans of other people in the environment.

SOLUTION SKILLS

Solution skills are communication skills that help people communicate more smoothly and assertively, primarily on the level of mind and thinking, in order to manage themselves and relationships with other people more effectively. They are focused on reasoning things through in a positive, constructive, and rational manner.

It is important to recognize that these skills involve putting simple attention on the skills and practicing them in a comfortable manner. It is not effective to concentrate intensely in applying the skills, and then become self-critical if you don't do them exactly right. The mind is very subtle and rarely functions at its best from trying to focus and concentrate hard. Straining to apply communication skills adds frustration and mental tension, which is in the opposite direction of helping to settle things down and develop the skills in an easy and natural way. This category of communication skills includes chapters on solution orienting, self-talking, reframing, decision making, solution building, negotiating, presenting, leading, and teaching.

CHAPTER 21
SOLUTION ORIENTING

 Solution orienting refers to attending to strengths, resources, and skills that support progress toward solutions, rather than focusing on problems.

1. It is quite important to face problems assertively, rather than non-assertively avoid or aggressively deny them. But how we face problems affects our ability to solve them. The more time and energy on problems, the bigger they become. We want solutions to expand and problems to shrink. Effective use of the mind involves gently directing attention toward positive solutions rather than problems. This is fundamental to how the mind works.

2. The communication skill of solution orienting involves focusing on strengths, resources, and practical skills people have inside themselves to create solutions. Actions are not thought of as successes and failures as much as feedback toward solutions that fulfill plans and goals. The focus is on what's working, going well, and can change, not on problems or failures.

3. Moving toward something implies moving away from something else. Included in a goal is what's wrong and needs to change. For example, a goal of improving your score includes the problem that the current score is not what you want. Focusing on goals and solutions uplifts the mind and heart, which strengthens problem solving ability. Focusing on problems, failures, and what's wrong can depress the mind. Solution orienting places attention on positive, constructive evaluations of actions and their results. But when strong emotions arise, attention needs first to be on allowing emotions to be expressed and settle down. Straining or moving quickly to try to solve things when emotions are strong rarely helps.

4. Solution orienting includes asking questions that assume a solution is available, and if possible even reframing the idea that there is a problem. It also includes negotiating solvable problems, emphasizing any small steps of progress, pursuing exceptions, looking for positive features in negative behavior, replacing the language of problems such as pathological terms with positive terms, and referring to problems as past and tentative while referring to solutions as upcoming and definite.[3]

5. An example of solution-orienting communication is the miracle question: 'If a miracle happens that solves the problem, then what will you do next?'[3] Also, the long view question can foster attention on solutions rather than problems: 'What will you be feeling about this 5, 10 (or 25) years from now?' These help avoid getting stuck on problems due to narrow-minded thinking.

6. In solution orienting, there is less analysis of the past to try to find the cause. A general understanding of the past is helpful, but focusing on it may result in getting

mired down in it, without ever finding the real cause. It is more effective to direct attention to the future when the problem is solved, rather than the past when it arose. The past can't change; but how the past is understood and its effects in the present can change, and this directly affects progress toward solutions. Establishing clear goals and plans is proactive and constructive. It is starting with the goal or end clearly in mind.

7. The skill of solution orienting involves basic orientation toward goals. Life energy naturally flows. It is easier to guide the flow in a positive direction than to stop it from flowing in a negative direction. Working on solutions is also much more enjoyable than struggling to end problems. Change occurs all the time, and in fact is inevitable. What is needed is to support the process of inevitable change toward solutions and progress. Even a small change can trigger change in a whole system such as a relationship, family, or company. Even a small step of progress is encouraging and uplifting.

8. Here are other practical examples of solution-oriented questions:
    'What do you want to accomplish?' 'What is your goal?'
    'What will you do different when you have solved things?'
    'What's going well and how are you making them happen?'
    'What will be the first signs of progress and who will notice?'
    'How can your past training be applied toward a solution now?'
    'What's different when things are going well?'
    'If something like this happened before, how did you get through it then?'[3]

9. Mind is subtler than body, and needs to be treated more subtly. Problem-focused approaches such as the disease-oriented medical model don't recognize the subtle nature of mind. These valuable physical approaches can have negative side effects of negative thinking that can actually retard healing. For example, defining rehabilitation as social skills and assertiveness training can be more productive than labeling someone with a chronic psychiatric disorder.

10. Modern medicine is starting to recognize the role of mind in creating health. Focusing on positive, natural inner strengths is the basis for preventative or health-oriented medicine. Approaches such as medications need to fit into a solution-oriented approach that also uses the mind's natural healing power. The placebo effect, related to the power of positive belief, actually may be one of the most powerful healing influences in many popular physical and mental health treatment approaches. Medicine is much more effective when it is health-oriented rather than disease-oriented. Daily living in a healthy, balanced way naturally prevents many of the issues that disease-oriented medicine addresses.

Examples of How to Use This Skill

EXAMPLE 1

Ineffective use: When Bobby, one of the best pitchers in his Babe Ruth league, has two rough games in a row, and this time the team gets their first loss, he asks the coach about it. The coach, who has few communication skills, says that everyone has bad days. The coach reflects on it further, 'You're a good athlete, but maybe another sport would be better for you. It could be that you just peaked early in baseball; we'll have to see over the rest of the season. We're a good team, and we'll win more games.'

Effective use: Bobby is quite upset about two mediocre performances in a row, the first time this has ever happened. But he decides he is tired already tonight, and that he needs to rest. This weekend he'll call the catcher on the team and go over with him the strong points in the game, and how he can learn to use different pitches more effectively.

EXAMPLE 2

Ineffective use: Ted sees that his daughter, Beth, is sitting in her room, sobbing because she just can't seem to come up with any ideas as to how to begin work on her new homework assignment about city planning. Ted tries to help by encouraging his daughter to focus on the solution, not on the problem. He says, 'Feeling down about it really won't help, Beth. Try to be positive, and think about how you will feel when you present your project and the teacher likes it. Let's focus on the first practical step of what needs to be done, such as maybe considering the size and lay of the land.' Because Beth is outputting emotions and is not ready to focus on solutions yet, the timing is off on Ted's well-intentioned help and he is overlooking her emotional state. Beth ends up feeling even more overwhelmed, and tells her father she just wants to be alone for a while.

Effective use: When Ted hears his daughter sobbing over her homework, he recognizes he needs to validate her emotions, let them be expressed, and then allow her to settle down. After she settles down, she asks her father how he thinks she should start on the project. He says he has never worked on a city planning project before and that she probably knows more than he does. He asks, 'In the homework assignment that you said the teacher really liked last term, do you remember how you approached it?' Beth remembers that the first thing she did was to talk to a neighbor who works in that field. Ted asks his daughter whether that strategy might work again for the current project. Beth says, 'I think what I'll do is call the city planning office at city hall.' Ted responds that it sounds like an excellent start.

EXAMPLE 3

Ineffective use: Robin has lived in a small town all her life and is somewhat frightened about a job prospect in Chicago. Her older brother, Jerome, feels she needs to be practical and make up her mind. He says, 'Robin, think of what you'll learn, and the good money you'll make, plenty for being able to visit home; it's better to think positively about it, rather than worry about your fears.' Robin gets annoyed by her brother's pushy way of trying to help her, as if he doesn't think she is capable of accomplishing things on her own.

Effective use: Jerome asks if Robin is a little frightened about leaving, and listens as she talks about it. Robin finally says, 'I need to think it through practically.' Jerome says, 'Would you like me to help by jotting down the points as you think of them and talk them through out loud?' Robin says, 'Yeah, thanks bro.' Jerome helps Robin come up with useful points, asking her if a particular point is important to her or not. The next day, she makes her decision and thanks him for the support, even though he realizes she made the decision on her own.

SUMMARY OF CHAPTER 21: Solution Orienting

1. Focusing on problems can make the problems seem bigger.
2. Solution orienting focuses on what works and is going well.
3. Orienting to solutions uplifts and strengthens mind and heart.
4. Solution orienting focuses attention on positive progress.
5. Knowing the cause of a problem is not necessary to solve it.
6. The past can't change, but how it affects us now can change.
7. Small changes can trigger changes in an entire system.
8. Solution orienting directs attention with subtle communication.
9. Mind is subtler than body and needs more refined approaches.
10. The mind is a powerful tool for creating health.

CHAPTER 22
SELF-TALKING

 Self-talking refers to communicating with oneself in a manner that supports healthy, positive, assertive thinking and minimizes negative thinking.

1. In the outward flow of energy, the heart's goals and the mind's plans are expressed in actions to change the environment. But if we don't plan effectively in the mind, the desired effects aren't produced, and then plans or goals need to be reevaluated. The mind shapes the heart's inner feelings into emotional behavior. Negative emotional behavior can result from negative evaluations or interpretations in the mind. A rising feeling of uncertainty can become a negative emotion of fear or a positive emotion of interest, depending on how the mind interprets the situation. The communication skill of self-talking relates to how the mind interprets goals, plans, actions, and the environmental circumstances.

2. Self-talking involves automatic habits of thinking about oneself that can support or interfere with effective action. Positive self-talk such as, 'Go ahead; you handle these situations well,' or, 'I'll focus very well on the task this time, or 'I'm going for it; at least I'll learn from it,' support improved performance. Positive self-statements foster balanced, assertive behavior.

3. Self-talking also can be negative and decrease successful action, such as: 'Clumsy me again; aren't I smart enough to walk yet?' or, 'I'm a lost cause.' Automatic negative thinking is related to what is called cognitive distortions or irrational beliefs, meaning that it twists understanding in a negative direction. Negative, self-critical thinking increases with non-assertiveness and is associated with feeling down, perfectionism, and also procrastination.

4. Aggressive behavior involves not enough planning and reevaluating in the mind. It is associated with not taking responsibility for one's own actions, and blaming others. The small amount of self-talking involved in this pattern is often very brief, and frequently very self-critical.

5. Negative self-talking is in the opposite direction of solution orienting. It usually involves some form of expanding the problem and shrinking the solution. Here are some examples of negative thinking habits: [4]

    - Magnifying negatives and minimizing positives, such as focusing on what could or should have been done rather than things done well.

    - Jumping to negative conclusions, such as assuming something bad about others, or predicting negative results without any facts.

- All-or-nothing thinking, such as things must be perfect or they are a complete failure.
- Internalizing blame and externalizing credit, such as blaming yourself for bad things you had no control over, or attributing good things you did have control over to the circumstances or to other people.
- Mislabeling, such as thinking you are a loser or are unworthy, as if the label was a permanent and complete description of who you are.

6. Another type of negative thinking about oneself is called emotional reasoning. This involves making evaluations about how things are in the environment based on current emotions. It is thinking that things must be bad because right now emotions are negative. An example of emotional reasoning is assuming people at a party are probably not good people, or it is wrong to be there, because at the moment you are unhappy or frustrated.

7. Positive self-talking supports assertive behavior to increase success and fulfillment. When there is a smooth flow of energy through heart, mind, and behavior, there is less need to re-evaluate, and self-talking tends to decrease.

8. Positive self-talking develops in the same way that any habit is developed. It involves building a new and healthier habit from the inside out, first working on the level of heart, then mind, and then emotions and other behavior. What we feel and how we think significantly influence our emotions and other behavior. Changing the self-talking in our minds directly will help change bodily reactions and emotional behavior.

9. On the level of heart and feelings, this involves making a general goal or desire of the new habit, and reminding yourself of it regularly. On the level of mind, it involves planning how to implement the new habit and re-evaluating behavior regularly. This includes identifying very clearly the new habit, even writing out a new self-statement, looking for instances to express it, and finding cues to help interrupt the old habit. On the level of emotional behavior, it involves catching the old negative habit when it comes up, placing attention on the new habit, and then comfortably practicing until the new positive habit is automatic. Attention to each level of the flow of energy—heart, mind, body, and behavior—and inserting a positive self-statement as early as you remember to do so, will develop the new positive habit. With practice, the old habit fades out without straining about it.

10. It generally is more helpful to emphasize developing new habits rather than changing old ones. In this solution-oriented approach, mistakes are seen as steps of progress in building the new habit. Their only significance is in helping you learn how to be more effective the next time the opportunity to use the positive habit arises.

Examples of How to Use This Skill

EXAMPLE 1

Ineffective use: Loren knows that he can be overly self-critical and makes a New Year's resolution to stop it because it is holding back his progress. Based on an old statement he remembers his high school coach saying, he comes up with a phrase to remind himself not to be down on himself, 'Life is too short to waste, so get out of the waste basket.'

Effective use: Loren feels that even with his New Year's resolution he has not progressed in reducing his self-critical habit, so he re-evaluates what he has been doing. He realizes his self-statement contains an old memory of frustration and failure associated with his dealings with his high school coach, who knew the sport well but didn't know how to empower his players. Loren tries out a more positive self-statement, 'I'm better prepared than I used to be, and learning with each new experience.' He is finding lately that he is just a little more willing to try out new approaches in his work. He has been considering taking a creativity course also.

EXAMPLE 2

Ineffective use: Judd feels that he is stuck at his job, doesn't really like any hobbies, is disgusted by the low quality of life he is barraged with on TV, and wants to get out of the rut in which he has found himself. He has come to the conclusion that he has to change his style of thinking and talking to himself. He decides that he will note down whenever he recognizes that he has negative thinking about his life, and then will go back at the end of each day to analyze where the thought came from and reasons he is so down on himself. After doing this for several days, he feels even more tired emotionally, and has not been sleeping well.

Effective use: Judd comes up with a plan to go to the mountain lodge that he found so beautiful on his trip last year. He will spend a long weekend going over his personal goals, and getting them clearer. From this experience, he will come up with some brief, general phrases to put on 3'X 5' cards and read them in the mornings when he wakes up, and then make a list of steps toward them he can do that day. He also simply reminds himself about the general goals before going to bed at night. He finds he is thinking less negatively, and that he feels a little more empowered and less stuck.

EXAMPLE 3

Ineffective use: Dan explains to his wife that he is not as social as she is, and frequently has a lousy time at house parties that she enjoys. They talk it over and come to an agreement that whenever Dan isn't feeling happy at these parties, he will signal to his wife and they will both go home, so he doesn't build up negative experiences and thinking about himself and others at the party. Over the next three months, they leave all but one party. Also, Dan's wife seems to be a little angrier and he feels she is unfairly blaming him for it. She also says she is kind of bored with her job, which she used to love.

Effective use: Dan and his wife talk about the people both of them are comfortable with, and also what things Dan feels he can talk with others about that are interesting to him. They join a book club together, as well as find people who have similar interests to Dan's. Dan also says that he will work on involving himself in conversations at house parties, and on finding something to entertain him when he is not feeling completely comfortable. His wife agrees to be more observant when Dan is really uncomfortable, and will return home with him on these occasions and focus on spending the evening in private conversation with him at home. The number of successful social events they attend slowly increases over the following months.

SUMMARY OF CHAPTER 22: Self-Talking

1. Self-talking involves making evaluations of one's own behavior.
2. Self-talking can involve automatic habits of thinking about oneself.
3. Negative thinking habits can be associated with non-assertiveness.
4. Aggressiveness involves very little, but very negative self-talking.
5. Negative self-talking is the opposite direction of solution orienting.
6. Emotional reasoning draws conclusions based on current emotions.
7. Self-talking usually decreases as assertive balance increases.
8. Positive self-talking develops from inner to outer levels.
9. Positive habits are built with clear goals, plans, and repeated action.
10. Emphasize building new habits rather than changing old habits.

CHAPTER 23
REFRAMING

 Reframing refers to changing a limiting viewpoint into a more positive and constructive alternative in order to foster progress toward goals.

1. Sometimes the approach taken in the mind leads to getting stuck in a pattern of thinking that hinders progress toward fulfilling goals and plans. The communication skill of reframing helps foster different ways of thinking that can reestablish progress.

2. When helping other people reframe their thinking, first summarize and validate to demonstrate you are listening and support current emotions. Only after you demonstrate you listened and accepted where they are at, and only after emotions have settled, will your practical suggestions be listened to and received positively by others.

3. Reframing then involves suggesting that a different way of considering the issue might be useful. If the person agrees to consider alternative ways to look at the issue, then you might ask what would be the consequences of considering a particular perspective. You might say, ' I wonder what would happen if the issue was looked at from the angle of ...' or, 'What would be the effect of approaching it from the standpoint that...' or, 'How would things change if...' or simply, 'What if...', and then briefly explain a new angle of approach. By now it is likely to be clear to do this only after emotions have settled down.

4. For example, let's say a teenager was acting macho, saying he might even fight another student for saying something derogatory. The coach might reframe the situation by suggesting that real strength involves maintaining emotional control and not getting thrown off balance, rather than losing control, giving away your inner power and giving in to beating on someone just because they called you a name.

5. One type of reframing that sometimes quickly results in more constructive ways of understanding an issue is called relabeling. This simply involves proposing a new label or term that redefines the issue and places it in a different context that is more constructive.

6. In the above example, it might be enough for the coach just to say, 'Maintaining emotional balance shows strength of character.' As another example, it might be helpful for a mother to relabel a cleaning chore her daughter calls 'a stupid waste of time' into 'a chance to exercise together, or 'a great opportunity to blow Grandma's mind.'

7. Sometimes the initial reaction to challenging situations is uncertainty or confusion; instead of assertiveness, there is hesitation to take action until the plan in

the mind has become clear. As the person begins to think through how to deal with the situation, however, the issues seem increasingly challenging, difficult, or hopeless. This is sometimes called catastrophizing. A useful reframe in this context is called normalizing. It involves placing something that is difficult into a more normal context that is easier to accept.

8. For example, if a mother was worrying a lot about her child having difficulty after a friend moved away, it might be a helpful reframe to point out that this is a common occurrence in healthy young children and is not by itself a sign of depression. If a friend was very concerned about an upcoming job interview, it might be helpful to point out that job interviews ordinarily are awkward at the start but become easier as the discussion moves into familiar areas such as past work experience. With this as well as all solution-focused skills, however, it is important that it be done at the right time, only after the person feels listened to and emotions have settled down.

9. Sometimes people can get stuck in negative emotions such as frustration, anger, sadness, boredom, or loneliness. There is the desire or goal to get out of the negative emotion, but not the plan about how to do it. Another type of reframing, called redirecting, is an important communication skill that can be used to deal with this type of situation. This involves changing the context by distracting the person's attention and directing it into some other activity. It may be as simple as asking for the person's opinion about a different topic, asking the person to help you with something, or just asking the person to go on a walk. The reframe is to change the overall situation in order to break the negative pattern. Redirecting attention and energy toward other plans or goals is effective for dealing with rejection, embarrassment, or unfairness. To succeed and flourish, even in another area, is a great way to deal with being stuck or blocked. As they say, success is the best revenge.

10. However, if a reframe doesn't seem to work and the person goes back to a negative viewpoint, it suggests that the person first needs to express emotions more. Under these circumstances, more summarizing, validating, empathizing, and disarming may be necessary in order to help things settle down to the point where reframing can be successful. Remember that dealing with the level of mind, such as with reframing, requires that emotions be settled down. Otherwise, people could feel not listened to, and it could escalate negative emotions rather than help people settle down to constructive rational thinking on the level of the mind.

Examples of How to Use This Skill

EXAMPLE 1

Ineffective use: One of Barbara's acquaintances she runs into at the mall tries to get her excited about a risky financial venture related to a new construction approach being tested in a beach town hit hard by a major storm. Barbara's husband wants to leave the mall to get to their daughter's volleyball match on time. He jumps into the conversation and says, 'It sounds more like crazy risk-taking to me than an investment opportunity.' Barbara gets annoyed, but stops the conversation and they leave to go to the match on time.

Effective use: Barbara's husband overhears a conversation she is having with a new acquaintance, and then says, 'This sounds like it needs to be thought through carefully based on more information. Honey, can we explore it further when we have more time, because the volleyball match will start in a few minutes, and I think we both really want to be there for her first match?' Barbara says to the acquaintance, 'Let's talk soon about this, when there's time to cover it properly. It's important for us to be there for our daughter. Sorry we have to rush off.'

EXAMPLE 2

Ineffective use: Little Stevie starts crying when the ice cream melts and falls off of his cone onto the ground. His mother says, 'Stop your crying, honey, you ate most of the ice cream anyway. And it'll be time for dinner soon. What kind of food do you want, Stevie? Do you want to go to Burger Hut? How about if we get a burger and fries with lots of catsup at Burger Hut, and you can get a free dinosaur cup for your soda?'

Effective use: When Little Stevie cries over his dropped ice cream, his mother recognizes that he is getting tired and a little cranky. She says, 'Your ice cream fell on the ground, and you're sad about it, right Stevie?' Stevie says, 'Yeah,' and continues to sob. 'Did you want to eat all the ice cream, and you're annoyed about it too?' Stevie says, 'Yeah, Mommy.' 'That can be frustrating.' He stops sobbing, and his mother further says, 'Can I help you with it?' Stevie says, 'Yeah, Mommy, it's a mess.' She says, 'Should we go pick up the ice cream and throw it in the trash can, do you see a trash can nearby, Stevie?' He says with some enthusiasm now, 'Mommy, that looks like a trash can over there.' She says, 'You're right, good job Stevie. Let's scoop the ice cream up and put it in the trash, so no one will slip and fall on it.' Stevie says, 'Okay, Mommy.' After they complete the clean-up, she says, 'Maybe we're both a little tired, let's go sit down a couple minutes, then we can decide what to see next.'

EXAMPLE 3

Ineffective use: Andy, a psychiatric nurse aide, runs to the snack room to respond to a patient who is yelling. He says, 'Hey, what's going on, Henry? Why are you yelling and disturbing everyone? Let's go to my office and talk about it. Settle down, pal.' Henry stops shouting, but won't move. Andy tries to walk him toward the office, but Henry pulls away and kicks the pop machine again. Andy decides to call for more help.

Effective use: Andy hurries to the snack room and says, 'Henry, you seem angry. What's happening? Would you please tell me about it?' Henry yells, 'I'm going to make this stupid thing pay back my money!' Andy says, 'Let's get your pop right away, Henry. What kind do you want? This machine must be broken. Henry grumbles, and Andy says, 'Let's go to the office to get change for your pop. Have you heard of other problems with the machine? We'll call to complain about the darn thing, if you want. I'd appreciate it if you'd settle down.' As they walk toward the office, Henry says it happened last week to someone else too. He is settling down quickly and the anger storm is averted. This builds trust between Henry and Andy, and no other staff members need to be called in for reinforcements.

SUMMARY OF CHAPTER 23: Reframing

1. Reframing involves thinking about an issue in a new way.
2. First show you understand the issue by summarizing and validating.
3. Suggest considering the effects of a different perspective on the issue.
4. Place emphasis on a deeper, more constructive approach to the issue.
5. Relabeling is using a label with more positive meanings.
6. Relabeling can change an issue from a negative to a positive context.
7. Catastrophizing creates negative contexts that are harder to deal with.
8. Normalizing is thinking of an issue in common or normal terms.
9. Redirecting involves quickly changing the direction of attention.
10. If reframing doesn't seem to be working, more listening is required.

CHAPTER 24
DECISION MAKING

 Decision making refers to coordinating heart's goals and requirements of the environment to plan behaviors that result in increased fulfillment.

1. The communication skill of decision making requires coordination of heart and mind for successful action in the environment. When decision making is weak or difficult, it is typically due to heart and mind not coordinating well with each other. The heart pulls in one direction—usually toward a sense of love—and the mind pulls in another direction—usually toward a sense of duty. When mutual decision making is difficult, frequently one person is considering it more from the heart and the other more from the mind.

2. The loving heart wants to unify things, and to be happy. Its role in decision making is to provide the overall purpose and motivation for action. When energy flows smoothly through the heart, it provides the goal and then supports the mind's job of planning, directing, and implementing action. A stressed heart results in non-assertiveness, inability to let go, inability to take action, or impulsive selfishness, harshness, and aggressiveness.

3. The dutiful mind wants to maintain balance in increasing happiness. It is concerned with doing the right thing. The mind's job is to make sure that unbounded love in the heart is expressed in healthy boundaries in behavior. For example, love is appropriately expressed differently to spouse, children, other family members, friends, or co-workers. The mind's role in decision making is to coordinate inner feelings with the outer environment, in order to plan and implement action. A stressed mind produces confused, weak thinking and ineffective action or fragmented thinking and inflexible action.

4. The deeper, more sensitive and powerful level of heart provides support for the more expressed level of mind. But the mind is the link between the inner heart and the outer environment. Its role is to guide action. The mind needs to make decisions rationally that guide healthy behavior. Emotions are rarely a successful basis for decision making. Emotions in the body, and also feelings in the heart, contribute effectively to decision making when they are more settled. If strong feelings and agitated emotions pull against the mind in evaluating duty and right action, they need to be given less importance in decision making. When input from the environment, what you feel, and how you think all match, then decisions are frequently effective. If they are not matching, then more settling down, input, and careful planning in the mind are needed.

5. The deepest, most refined feelings are associated with the inner sense of intuition. This helps decision making when these deep levels are not over-shadowed by stress. As body, mind, and heart become stress-free, the intuitive sense naturally gives reliable input in decision making. But when the deep feeling level is noisy and not stress-free, intuition can be unreliable. Under these common circumstances, the mind needs to evaluate input from the level of feeling carefully, before acting. Assuming intuition is right because it comes from the heart can result in unhealthy, ineffective decisions.

6. Healthy decisions involve clear thinking in an atmosphere of love and respect for self and others. First take time to settle down your own body, mind, and heart. Listen to input from the environment, using skills to help others settle down so they provide clearer signals. Listen to the fine feeling level of your heart, and clarify goals. Then use your mind to consider input from both your heart and the environment, and let your mind plan and direct timely action to accomplish the heart's goals.

7. It is appropriate to consider both short-term and long-term results of actions. With growth to higher levels of personal fulfillment, naturally concern for our families, communities, and society as a whole are the priority, due to the increased coordination of heart and mind for duty and right action. Decisions based only on short-term effects are typically regretted later when long-term effects begin to show up clearly.

8. In considering long-term effects of actions, input and guidance from reliable sources can help. Experienced elders in the family or community, scientifically-validated facts, the laws of the land, and religious texts that are traditional sources of information on right and wrong behavior all frequently offer helpful long-term perspectives that otherwise might be overlooked.

9. Prioritizing and cost/benefit analysis also can be helpful. Prioritizing is sorting actions from most to least important. Cost/benefit analysis is listing and comparing benefits and costs, both short-term and long-term. It can help to categorize decisions into small and big ones; make small decisions quickly, and take more time on big ones.

10. It is important not to get stuck in the process of decision making such that timely action is not taken. It isn't possible to take into account all potential effects of actions. Carefully plan in the time allowed, but then decide, take action, and accept the consequences. Repeating the cycle of feelings, thoughts, behaviors, and evaluating results builds skill in goals, plans, and actions that bring higher levels of fulfillment. These guidelines may seem simple, but carefully applying them helps effective decision making.

Examples of How to Use This Skill

EXAMPLE 1

Ineffective use: Colin is trying to make a difficult decision about whether to go to college or whether to buy a new car. He decides he will check out two of the potential colleges first, and explore student loan programs. While riding around with his best friend from hi school, his friend notices several nice cars at a used car dealership—including one he knows Colin likes—and enthusiastically says to stop and take a look. The used car dealer gets them to try out the car, and after an hour of working on Colin, the dealer gets Colin to sign on the line based on a special financing package.

Effective use: That night Colin enjoys cruising in his new car, but also feels a bit down about not being able to afford college at least for the next year. Colin talks to his mother and his uncle about the situation. He checks out one of the colleges nearby, and likes it. He decides to discuss the situation with the owner of the car dealership, asking his uncle to come along. Together they work a budget that would allow him to get a good car that he likes; it is not as flashy as the first one, but it fits in with his college budget.

EXAMPLE 2

Ineffective use: Sally and Lane have difficulty making even small decisions. They get a call from a good friend with an opportunity for two free tickets to go to a concert. They have previous plans to visit Sally's mother the same evening as the concert, and tell their friend that they need to think about it. After a day, they talk about it again, but can't seem to come up with a decision, and are hesitant to bring up to Sally's mother whether rescheduling is a possibility. The next day they decide to write down the pros and cons of both possibilities, and then think more about it. They decide to go to the concert, and call Sally's mother with the explanation that they may just stay home because Lane has been working late that week. When they finally call their friend back, the friend's schedule has changed and the tickets are no longer available. When they call Sally's mother, she also says she invited her neighbor instead. Sally and Lane both get angry that no one seems to consider their wishes and just go ahead with their lives without really caring about what Sally and Lane feel.

Effective use: Sally and Lane call her mother and ask about a possible change of plans, explaining that they have the chance for free tickets to a concert by a band they've never thought they'd have a chance to see. When the mother finds out who it is, she calls up and gets a ticket also, and they all have fun together at the concert—which completely surprises Sally.

EXAMPLE 3

Ineffective use: Audrey and Paul want to marry after Audrey finishes her degree. One of her advisors, a professor at another university who has been going through a long divorce, invites her to work for two months on a research project in Malaysia that could help her thesis. She could also visit relatives in Singapore on the trip. For years she has had an intuition she would go on such a trip. On the trip, she gets emotionally involved with the professor. On her return, she is very hurt to find that Paul reevaluates their marriage plans based on what has happened.

Effective use: Audrey openly discusses the professor's offer with Paul. Paul works out a plan with his company to go too. When Audrey brings up this possibility to the professor, he replies that things have changed and it may be necessary for one of his colleagues with research expertise to go instead. Audrey and Paul decide to go to Singapore for their honeymoon.

SUMMARY OF CHAPTER 24: Decision Making

1. Decision making requires good coordination of heart and mind.
2. The loving heart gives the overall purpose to the mind about behavior.
3. The dutiful mind is responsible to direct and implement behavior.
4. The heart gently guides the mind, but the mind guides behavior.
5. Intuition becomes more reliable as deep stress is eliminated.
6. Consideration of long-term and short-term effects helps decision making.
7. Reliable, traditional sources can help in evaluating long-term effects.
8. Decide as best as you can in the available time, but then take action.
9. Use of simple strategies helps decision making be more effective.
10. The cycle of deciding, acting, and evaluating builds decision making skill.

CHAPTER 25
SOLUTION BUILDING

 Solution building refers to settling down emotions, clarifying goals, deciding on and implementing a plan, and evaluating the results.

1. When the heart's goal seems to be blocked for some reason and the situation is challenging to resolve, applying a systematic strategy can help. The communication skill of solution building is an effective strategy that follows the cycle of feeling, thinking, and behavior. This process involves building a solution space by settling down emotions, developing a goal and plan by outlining solutions and locating one to try out, putting the plan into action, and evaluating the results by comparing them with the goal.

2. Solution building requires a rational state of mind that is not distracted by strong emotions. Solution building fundamentally is a two-stage process. The first stage is to settle down emotions. This is done by applying listening and emotion management skills. Only when emotions have settled down can solution building proceed effectively. Ignoring this first step is the reason many attempts to help others fix problems are ineffective and result in miscommunication.

3. The second stage is to develop and implement a solution. If you propose a solution and others reject it right away, the first stage of solution building—settling emotions and creating a solution space—was not adequately done. Building a solution also involves identifying goals, and then identifying means to implement the goals. Directing attention toward solutions once emotions have settled down, rather than focusing on problems, can reduce problems.

4. Here is a solution building model with the acronym SOLVE that is a simple framework for working toward a solution. It is based on the cycle of feeling, thinking, and behavior associated with goals, plans, actions, and evaluation of results.

S	Settle emotions	*Settle body, mind, and heart—inner silence*
O	Organize goal	*Clearly state problem—goal*
L	Locate solution	*Brainstorm solutions and pick one—plan*
V	Validate solution	*Define success and test solution—plan and act*
E	Evaluate results	*Review success—evaluate goal, plan, action*

5. **Settle emotions.** Effective solution building is based on establishing and maintaining an inner state in which heart, mind, and body listen to each other. This establishes a solution space that is the platform for creative solutions. In this assertively balanced space, energy flows more smoothly to express goals and plans in effective action.

6. ***Organize goal.*** Identifying the goal to be achieved is an important step. This is basically a process of discussing the positive outcomes to be achieved, and establishing goals that people can mutually accept and agree on.

7. ***Locate solution.*** This step involves brainstorming, thinking openly and creatively without trying to evaluate how practical the ideas are, until several possible solutions have been developed. Then consider each one, anticipating likely short-term and long-term results, and identifying one solution that seems to fit best. Frequently this involves identifying several issues, then prioritizing them from least to most important or easiest to most difficult. It is easier to start with a simple issue to build experience and confidence, then work on more challenging issues. Challenging issues can be addressed by breaking them down into smaller and more easily solvable parts, then putting the parts back together to address the original, more challenging issue.

8. ***Validate solution.*** This step involves actually implementing the plan. It includes defining how to implement the solution and how to decide whether the solution worked. Identify the steps to try out the solution. Then specify the outcome that will indicate how well the solution worked.

9. ***Evaluate results.*** This step involves checking the actual results with the plan and goal. It may include feeling satisfied the issue was solved, deciding to try out another solution, or redefining the goal or plan based on the information gained from testing the solution.

10. In today's society many people are in too much of a hurry to try to fix things, which can interfere with finding effective solutions. There is inadequate recognition of how heart, mind, body, and emotions relate to each other and systematically work together for healthy, effective action. Not enough attention is placed first on establishing a rational solution space as the platform for coming up with solutions to challenges. It is especially important to recognize that one of the biggest drawbacks to effective solutions is not taking the time to settle down emotions first. When this is done patiently and consistently, solutions come more quickly, effectively, naturally, and profoundly. As a general guideline, the deeper the settling down, the more inner quietness and silence, the clearer the feeling and thinking processes are, and the more effective and powerful the goals, plans, and actions will be.

Examples of How to Use This Skill

EXAMPLE 1

Ineffective use: Tracy has to decide whether to stay at her job and report to human resources about harassment by other women with whom she works, or just to leave and find another job. In talking about it with her neighbor friend, the neighbor pulls out a piece of paper and starts making a list of the concerns about the decision Tracy has. At some point her neighbor gets frustrated and says that it is taking too long and Tracy is too indecisive. Tracy and her neighbor end up in an argument about other matters, which ends with them not talking to each other for three months.

Effective use: After thinking about the issue over the weekend, Tracy realizes that her concern about whether to leave her job also involves several other important concerns in her life, including her long wish to go on an extended vacation. Over the next month, she writes down several key issues about her life, thinks through the most important ones and prioritizes them. She then decides to visit her aunt, who she deeply respects. Her aunt helps her go through a systematic procedure to address the three most significant issues. With her aunt's patient support and good listening skills, Tracy decides on a strategy that she feels very confident about, and begins to implement the first one. This involves finding out about two other possible careers, and also checking into programs in her company for educational training support. She also decides to work with the human resource development staff to build assertiveness skills in dealing with co-workers.

EXAMPLE 2

Ineffective use: Raul's father is getting older and is at a point in his life when he needs more assistance in daily living. Raul doesn't really want to move to the town where his father lives and leave his current life and decent job, but the family cannot afford an assisted-living home for his father—who would refuse to go anyway. Raul talks to his youngest brother at length and eventually gets him to move in with his father, since he already lives in the same town. But his brother feels pressured by the situation and expresses anger at Raul for kind of forcing him to do it.

Effective use: As the eldest child, Raul recognizes his obligation to help lead the family in coming up with a plan to help his father. He talks to his siblings and they agree to meet together to begin working on the issue. Raul lays out a series of steps—the SOLVE approach—to develop a plan that will be tried. After two meetings with his siblings and their father, a plan is worked out that they all agree to test out for three months. Their father is grateful for the display of family unity and support, and the respect for his own wishes.

EXAMPLE 3

Ineffective use: Annemarie feels she needs to respond immediately after being told by her firm's biggest client that they are considering going with a national firm. She wants a coherent proposal that satisfies the client's needs for both regional and national expertise, and calls for an emergency meeting the morning after a major hurricane threat in the area, which rekindled strong emotions among the staff about moving the corporate offices. She tries to get her staff to focus on their creative strategies program which they trained in recently at considerable expense to the company, but they end up bickering about moving the offices. She calls off the meeting, gets annoyed about the situation, and decides just to put together her own ideas.

Effective use: Annemarie starts the emergency meeting by allowing her staff to express frustrations about the early morning time, as well as concerns about the hurricane close call the night before. After about 10 minutes, the emotional tension in the room seems to settle down. There is agreement for a special meeting at the end of the month to begin dealing with the office location issue. After a short break, she then outlines the overall importance and purpose of the meeting. Staff members express their feelings about it, and then they begin working as a team, using a solution building approach, and also using the new creative strategies program. They come up with a solid strategy that involves collaboration with three firms from other regions in order to provide the client with national coordination of services.

SUMMARY OF CHAPTER 25: Solution Building

1. Solution building uses the cycle of feelings, thoughts, and actions.
2. The first stage of solution building is to settle down emotions.
3. The second stage is to develop and implement a plan of action.
4. SOLVE is a simple, systematic solution building strategy.
5. Solution building involves maintaining assertive balance.
6. Specify clearly what the problem or issue is that is to be solved.
7. Brainstorm solutions and identify one to test.
8. Define how to evaluate the solution and then implement it.
9. Evaluate the success of the results in terms of the original issue.
10. Settling down emotions first yields quicker and more effective solutions.

CHAPTER 26
NEGOTIATING

 Negotiating refers to communicating cooperatively with people to build agreements that are mutually beneficial and that increase trust.

1. Frequently people want to be part of the process of decision making and don't want to accept decisions imposed by others. Undoubtedly you will find many situations in which people may not accept your decisions, or you may not accept the decisions of others. Negotiating is an important skill to help people work together toward mutual agreements.

2. The communication skill of negotiating is most effective between people who assert their own goals and plans while respecting the goals and plans of others. This is called a win-win negotiation strategy, in which people agree from the outset to work toward mutually beneficial agreements. It promotes trust and interest in maintaining relationships for continuing mutual benefit.

3. People who negotiate in a non-assertive manner engage in a lose-win strategy. They tend to give in to avoid conflict. Later they may feel taken advantage of and resentful. This can build up stress, resulting in health and other problems, or that spills out in aggressive anger outbursts.

4. People who are aggressive negotiators typically engage in a win-lose strategy. They spend lots of energy fighting in order to win, sometimes misrepresenting or hiding information to slant things their way, which inevitably harms relationships when others find out the actual situation. The longer-term effects include personal guilt, defensiveness, criticism or rejection by others, increased difficulty building relationships based on trust, and even material greed in an attempt to replace the lack of healthy, fulfilling relationships—trying to fill the emptiness due to unhealthy relationships with material possessions. This is unfortunately a common, counterproductive lifestyle in our world family.

5. The communication skill of negotiating involves the basic sequence of outer to inner in order to develop the proper platform for mutually assertive communication. Then it involves the inner to outer sequence to develop mutual goals, plans, and actions to create a mutually fulfilling agreement. First settle emotions, then build mutual respect, learn each other's wants, develop mutual goals, and plan together how to implement the agreement.

6. Here is a simple model of negotiating, using the acronym AGREE:

    A *Access assertive balance.* Use grounding and listening skills to settle your own and the other person's emotions.

    G *Generate respect.* Use disarming, validating, and empathizing to connect with each other as individuals.

    R *Recognize goals.* Identify each other's short-term and long-term goals and interests.

    E *Evoke mutual goals.* Build goals and sub-goals beneficial to both.

    E *Establish concrete plans and actions.* Work together to identify specific steps to implement mutually beneficial agreements.

7. There is the issue that seems to place people on opposing sides, and there is the relationship between the people involved. Dealing with the relationship first establishes the basis of cooperation that facilitates working together.[5] It especially involves applying the skills that deal with settling down emotions, such as disarming and validating. It includes putting yourself in the other person's shoes, or empathizing, acknowledging and accepting emotions, allowing frustration to be expressed using the skill of venting as necessary, not reacting to emotional outbursts, and not trying to make others wrong.

8. Negotiating involves solution building skills to develop ways to narrow down differences, once teamwork has been established. It becomes an opportunity for mutual creative expression that can be very enjoyable, rather than grueling, vicious, unhealthy competition resulting in success or failure.

9. The key to healthy negotiating is to define the task as finding a mutually beneficial agreement—mutually beneficial outcomes. This places both parties on the same side and makes it easier to work together. From the same side, they can look at the issue from similar angles. Energies flow in the same direction toward agreement, rather than mixing up the issue with the relationship and having opposing energies.

10. Defining the task of negotiating as trying to prevail over the other person and make them give in interferes with long-term success. It places people on opposing sides. Opposing others rarely works well, is a waste of energy, and damages relationships. It uses up energy on struggling against the other person, and this energy is not available to be applied for creative solutions. The short-term gain may look worthwhile, but it doesn't consider the bigger picture. When long-term results of a more stressful and suspicious world are factored in, it is a lose-lose result for everyone, including society as a whole. The dissatisfaction and strain on relationships creates more tension, less trust, and deeper divisions that don't produce long-term results toward permanent happiness and fulfillment in life.

Examples of How to Use This Skill

EXAMPLE 1

Ineffective use: As a buyer for a large department store chain, Jocelyn feels she is a good negotiator. She thinks quickly in debating with potential venders, and she usually finds a way to get what she considers to be the best deal on behalf of her company. In the past five years, however, she has found it difficult in her private life to maintain a long-term relationship, and also to some degree with business suppliers. She wants to get married and begin a family, but is confused that many of the skills she feels are so successful in her work seem to backfire in relationships. She is increasingly cynical toward men, who don't appreciate her communication skills, and who in her opinion are arrogant, aloof, and frequently incompetent.

Effective use: Jocelyn decides that she might waste less time in evaluating new relationships if she spends the first couple of dates watching how her date treats other people, and listening deeply to questions about the direction in life that the man wants to go. She finds in doing this that she is clearly not interested in some of them, but that the few she may have an interest in are much more willing to talk about long-term plans and goals. She seemed never to be able to get men to consider these issues with her before; and she is finding that she can learn a lot, and get a deeper feeling about others, by taking the time to listen more carefully to their thoughts and feelings.

EXAMPLE 2

Ineffective use: Harry and his cousin, Steve, both have claim to a 30-acre plot of land from their grandparents' estate. Steve wants to build a house and raise horses; Harry wants to build several houses for profit. They try to talk it through, Steve saying his grandfather loved horses and Harry saying there was nothing in the will about keeping the land for horses. They end up having a big shouting match, with both refusing to talk to each other for over five years.

Effective use: On a camping trip, Harry and Steve talk over their dreams. Harry wants a lakeside cabin; Steve wants to raise horses. They decide together to apply the AGREE model to negotiate with each other. Together they decide to build six houses on the acreage, five to sell. Harry will get all the profit, and Steve will get one of the houses and the remaining land to raise horses. They have great fun teasing each other while working together. Now Steve's family visits Harry at the lake a couple times a year.

EXAMPLE 3

Ineffective use: In beginning a new job in sales at a regional company, Wiley notices the high amount of territoriality and competitive jealousy among sales staff. He decides the only way he can function in this environment is to get clear directions and arrangements from the sales manager about his area, and generally to keep quiet about his strategies.

Effective use: Wiley begins to realize that if he continues in the direction based on his initial evaluation of the company atmosphere, he will soon not like the job and will want to leave. He decides to try a new strategy that involves talking with the three sales reps in areas adjacent to his, and trying to work something out that would be mutually beneficial. Together he and the other three reps come up with some sales approaches that have never been tried, and that open up small but meaningful new market segments. He also starts to build trusting friendships with these colleagues.

SUMMARY OF CHAPTER 26: Negotiating

1. Healthy negotiating helps people achieve mutual goals.
2. An assertive, win-win style of negotiating is most effective.
3. Lose-win negotiating is non-assertive and fosters resentment.
4. Win-lose negotiating is aggressive and fosters poor relationships.
5. Negotiating involves outer to inner, and then inner to outer levels.
6. AGREE is a simple and effective model for negotiating.
7. Deal with the relationship first to establish a platform for agreement.
8. Negotiating builds opportunities for mutual creative expression.
9. The key is to define the task as cooperating, not opposing.
10. The longer-term result of opposing is a lose-lose situation.

CHAPTER 27
PRESENTING

 Presenting refers to communicating thoughts and feelings to groups of people in a manner that promotes understanding and acceptance.

1. You probably have sat through presentations that required lots of will power to avoid falling asleep or running out for some fresh air. These presentations are usually due to not enough preparation. The communication skill of presenting will help you convey thoughts and feelings to groups of people more comfortably and effectively.

2. An important point to remember is that time is precious. People appreciate your respect for their time. It is important to talk about things you know about and can talk about concisely, which requires preparation. The key is first to identify the overall point you want to make. Plan clear answers to who, what, how, when, and where. Notes will keep you on track during a talk and protect from wasting time by rambling or drifting into other topics.

3. Whether it is a short 2-4 minute talk or an hour-long speech, it will be easier for listeners to follow if it is structured in a sequence of a few key points that are repeated in the presentation. A famous guideline is, "Say what you will say, say it, and then say what you said."

4. Here is a basic structure for presentations that is based on the sequence of the heart's goal, mind's plan, and body's action, and then summary (GPAS):

   G *Goal.* Smile, describe the value for the audience of your talk through establishing the need, purpose, or goal by introducing an interesting, humorous, or important fact or question to inspire them. Then state in one sentence the overall main point you want to say.

   P *Plan.* Briefly outline the sequence of points you will make that will explain in more detail the overall main point.

   A *Action.* Explain each point, first in general and then by concrete example.

   S *Summary.* Briefly summarize the points if time allows, but at least restate the need and the single overall main point that addresses the need, and then thank your listeners.

5. It is important to think through who your listeners will be and to plan how to help them understand. This involves using words and examples that respect the cultures and interests of the group, starting your talk from their level of knowledge of the topic, and being open-hearted and appreciative of any questions people ask in trying to understand you.

6. It is your responsibility to be clear, not your listeners' responsibility to figure out what you are trying to say. Most likely you will know more about the topic than your listeners. It is thus usually helpful to use simple words, short sentences, and present only two or three main points. TV commercials are usually only 25-50 seconds long, in part because of the average attention span and length of short-term memory (as well as the outrageous costs).

7. It is very important to make it easy for your listeners to follow what you are saying. For example, it is helpful to guide listeners through your presentation with comments such as, "The second point is..." or "This is important because..." or "The point is..." Also, it is important to talk loud and clear for listeners to hear you, and if necessary to move to where they can see you. Make sure people in the back row can hear and see you. Checking ahead of time to be sure that any audio, video, and lighting equipment is set up properly and works is very important. Be very familiar with the equipment, or have someone else operate it.

8. The communication skill of presenting involves use of body language that is consistent with your speech. Smiling, direct eye contact with your listeners, speaking a little slower than usual, open postures, avoiding repeating the same gestures a lot, and brief pauses between points can all strengthen the presentation. Timing is essential to good presenting.

9. People are usually willing to listen to a presenter who is respectful and genuine even if the presentation has some mistakes and is not very smooth. Genuineness comes from making a sincere attempt to communicate without trying to act as if you have qualities, skills, experience, or knowledge you don't have. Perhaps the single most effective way to ensure this is to be honest with your listeners and present what you believe to be true.

10. Public speaking is frequently identified as one of the most anxiety-provoking experiences. Use of grounding skills prior to the presentation can settle down your emotions and help you get through the initial anxiety. It is also helpful to recognize that most everyone feels nervous about public speaking. Audiences are so used to speakers being a bit nervous that in many cases it isn't an issue at all. One of the most useful aids to increase your confidence and lower anxiety is to practice your talk several times first.

Examples of How to Use This Skill

EXAMPLE 1

Ineffective use: Greg knows he will be asked to say something at his neighbor's wedding party, but he doesn't like public speaking, and thinking about it just seems to make him more anxious. He decides that the best thing to do is just to get up and speak from the heart. At the reception, what comes up is a story about how his neighbor came home very late and mistakenly parked his car in Greg's garage rather than his own garage. The story didn't go over well, and his neighbor was somewhat embarrassed and frustrated by Greg's speech.

Effective use: Greg wants to speak from the heart at his neighbor's wedding party, so he thinks about it and comes up with two short stories about his neighbor's kindness to him. He tells the stories to some other friends, and it seems to go well. He decides he doesn't need to write anything down, but feels he can spontaneously tell the stories briefly and in a way that illustrates the good qualities of his neighbor.

EXAMPLE 2

Ineffective use: Paul has the reputation of being a very accomplished motivational speaker. But at his son's high school graduation party, he forgets who his audience is. He tells some of his best stories, ending up talking for over 15 minutes, which is a short talk compared to his usual speaking engagements. During the talk, his son and a group of friends walk out into the hallway, and after a while begin laughing loud. Later that day he complains about it to his son, who replies that his father went on and on, making the party about his own life, not about his son's graduation.

Effective use: Georgina wants to make a presentation at the family annual Thanksgiving dinner about the possibility of the family going in together to buy a vacation home at the lake. She knows that it is challenging for issues to be brought up at the dinner, because it gets a little boisterous and everyone is engaged in their own conversations. Even though it will be an informal setting, she decides to create a clear and concise talk that follows the formula for presenting that she has learned. She hones it down to three key points, and her entire presentation of two minutes is listened to carefully and generates considerable constructive discussions during the evening. Family members ask her to pursue the idea, and to write a letter to them summarizing her research as the basis for taking the idea to the next stage of implementation.

EXAMPLE 3

Ineffective use: James is especially interested in the history of radio equipment. He is invited to give a 20-minute talk at the local senior center, and he brings his prized wooden radio collection. As he starts the talk, someone asks how radios really work. By the time James finishes explaining the basic physics of radio waves, he is asked to stop so people can have lunch on time. He feels angry about being cut off and disappointed about not being able to present his radio collection.

Effective use: James thinks of his audience before the talk, and anticipates someone might ask how radios work. He decides that at the beginning of his talk he will describe clearly what he will cover. He will say that he's happy after lunch to describe how radios work for anyone interested in learning about it, but not in his talk. He gives his talk, with a little history of each radio in the collection. At the end, he again says he is available after lunch to answer detailed questions about radios. Three people talk to him after lunch, and he feels happy about the experience of giving the talk and getting positive feedback and interest in his collection.

SUMMARY OF CHAPTER 27: Presenting

1. Effective presentations require proper preparation.
2. Talk about things you know about, and be brief.
3. Effective presentations follow a planned structure and sequence.
4. Give the need, the wholeness, the details, and summarize.
5. Speak to your listeners' knowledge level and use familiar examples.
6. Use simple words, short sentences, and present only 2-3 main points.
7. Use guideposts that help guide listeners' through your presentation.
8. Use body language that is consistent with the content of your talk.
9. Genuineness and honesty make up for presentation mistakes.
10. A very useful way to deal with anxiety is to practice your talk first.

CHAPTER 28
LEADING

 Leading refers to inspiring and guiding people to work toward healthy goals and plans that result in increased mutual fulfillment and betterment of the world.

1. What is inside heart and mind naturally is expressed outside in emotions, speech, and other behavior. Each feeling, thought, and action influences the environment. In leadership roles, what is inside gets broadcast outside, magnified by the attention of other people and by drawing out similar qualities in them. Healthy and unhealthy qualities both get amplified.

2. Role modeling is fundamental to the communication skill of leading. Being a good role model means living how you encourage others to live. Followers want to trust leaders, and they carefully observe leaders' actions. People who are honest to themselves and others, take responsibility for their own emotions and actions, maintain assertive balance, protect themselves from fatigue and stress, and are fulfilled enough in themselves to act spontaneously for the good of others meet the basic requirements for leaders.

3. The communication skill of leading involves applying communication skills to enliven healthy feelings and thoughts within people and foster their smooth expression for successful action. To do this, leaders have to know what to do and how to do it. The skill of leading requires clear goals, sometimes called vision. Leaders respect the power and trust given by family, friends, co-workers, or other members of society. They promote worthy, attainable goals that consider long-term as well as short-term consequences. The purpose and value of the goals need to be expressed clearly so others can understand them and relate to them as their own goals.

4. The communication skill of leading also involves identifying clear plans that are practical steps of how to achieve the goal or vision. It requires flexibility to change plans according to changing circumstances, while maintaining consistent focus and direction on the mutual goals to be achieved.

5. Leading communicates commitment to goals through action that demonstrates how to work toward the goal in a focused manner. Leading is not only on the level of speech, but also requires active participation in implementing goals and plans in action. Leaders inspire responsible action for the good of society through their own responsible actions.

6. Leading importantly includes the skills of listening, validating, and empowering. Followers need to be shown they are respected and valued. This involves believing in the abilities of others, listening and supporting them, and using their talents and creativity to improve plans and actions. It also involves asking for and being

receptive to other opinions, considering their value, and allowing others to share in planning. It rarely involves harshly criticizing, demeaning, looking down at others, or related ways to impose a fear-based 'I am the boss' atmosphere of restrictive control. These frequently undermine teamwork and result in resentment, passive resistance, and eventually defiant opposition. Effective leaders observe carefully when to be authoritarian, democratic, laid back, or mentoring in leadership style.

7. An important part of leading is giving directions about how to do something. It involves using words and actions that are consistent, clear and specific. Verbal and non-verbal behaviors need to be congruent and signal the same thing. If you tell people you are happy with their performance, but your body language signals anger, then the messages don't match. This can be very confusing. Brief, specific, and consistent directions increase clarity. It is often helpful to request the listener restate directions to verify that you have communicated them accurately. You can then clarify any inaccuracies, respond to questions, and give additional explanation. Giving feedback includes regularly reporting progress toward goals, and also recognizing accomplishments with praise and recognition to keep things on track.

8. Leading applies the skill of solution orienting. The focus is on moving toward goals rather than getting lost in problems, but listening and validating any strong emotions first. It involves the strength to admit mistakes quickly, but also not get overwhelmed such that the goal is lost.

9. Leaders need to minimize getting too busy and hurried. When this occurs, the subtle feelings of mutual respect and appreciation between leader and followers are eroded in the mistaken attempt at efficiency. An aggressive style emerges that contributes to resentment in followers, leading to opposition and sometimes undermining of constructive relationships. This is an unfortunate and all-to-common pattern in organizations and governments.

10. Friendliness, compassion, showing genuine interest, treating people as important individuals, taking time to mentor people on an individual basis, and expressing happiness all reflect leadership skills. Charisma, the ability to charm and inspire, also can be very beneficial for leaders. But it needs to be backed up with assertive balance, respect for others, maturity, and honesty. Charismatic individuals who do not meet the basic requirements to lead described above have a disintegrating and destructive influence that misleads and weakens the entire society.

Examples of How to Use This Skill

EXAMPLE 1

Ineffective use: Barbara feels she has learned a lot about relationships, because she has had so many. She has had first-hand experience and insight into the ways partners can undermine relationships by not having certain practical skills. She wants to be known as someone with special skills in relationships, and she feels the way to do this is to write a book and give seminars on it. Even though she realizes that she hasn't been very successful establishing long-term relationships herself, she feels she is a natural leader, and can help people in marital consulting. Her book advises people to follow their hearts, and not to get stuck in situations such as a marriage that isn't satisfying after really trying hard.

Effective use: Barbara recognizes that she doesn't know how to build a permanent marriage, because she hasn't been able to achieve it, even though she has been trained in many of the skills that so-called experts propound. However, she also recognizes she has lots of success and experience in the basics of how to meet new people and present herself that creates positive first impressions. She decides to write a book about these topics, which brings her success. She directs questions about other aspects of relationships she has not mastered to other people, and this honesty endears her to others.

EXAMPLE 2

Ineffective use: Eduardo and Katie are deeply in love with each other and want to start a family. Neither of them feels that they were raised very effectively by their own parents, who in Katie's case were overprotective and in Eduardo's case were just too busy. They want to take time for their children, and to make their children feel much loved. They are confident that their love alone will be the best role model for their children and ensure a successful family life.

Effective use: Both Katie and Eduardo recognize that their own families didn't provide the best models of parenting. They know they do have the most important thing, which is taking the time to show their love to their children in caring and nourishing them. They also recognize that parenting involves considerable skill in training and supervision. They both decide to take a year and volunteer at community child care services, and to take several training programs together to develop skills that were missing in their own families, and then to plan together how they want to raise and lead their children.

EXAMPLE 3

Ineffective use: Mr. Jefferson is known for his very high intelligence, ambition, and charisma. By using some communication skills, and by carefully managing his public image, he has become a prominent leader. Focusing on outer image and not also on inner balance, however, he has not developed personal qualities consistent with his public image. He misuses his power, manipulates people around him, attempts to hide it to protect his image, and ends up creating confusion, divisiveness, cynicism, and mistrust that is not in the best interests of society.

Effective use: Mr. Jefferson recognizes that, even with his high talents, he doesn't yet meet basic requirements of being a healthy role model needed for public leadership. He retires from public life and begins an extensive study of great leaders, noting carefully their personal behavior, reflections about themselves, and legacies. He finds a positive relationship between personal honesty, healthy influence on others, and personal happiness. He redirects his life to this higher understanding of leadership, writes very successfully about it, and builds a well-deserved and positive national reputation.

SUMMARY OF CHAPTER 28: Leading

1. What is inside heart and mind is expressed in speech and action.
2. Role modeling is fundamental to the skill of leading.
3. Leading requires vision, which involves very clear goals.
4. Leading requires clear plans and flexibility to change as needed.
5. Leading is not only through speech, but also concrete action.
6. Listening, validating, and empowering are important to leading.
7. Leading applies the skill of solution orienting.
8. Leaders listen to others and give regular, positive feedback.
9. Leaders are careful not to get too busy and in a hurry.
10. The power to lead must be accompanied by maturity and honesty.

CHAPTER 29
TEACHING

 Teaching refers to communicating information with clarity and interest that helps people access knowledge and apply it to fulfill their own goals and plans.

1. Teaching is a very important communication skill requiring integration of heart and mind, assertive balance, openness, patience, clear knowledge of the subject, enthusiasm, and a sense of humor. Attending, engaging, listening, emotion management, decision making, solution building, respecting, empowering, motivating, negotiating, mediating, and presenting skills are all needed. The skill of teaching also could be placed in the next section on the level of heart, but the mind is a bit more emphasized in teaching.

2. Being a good example is basic to effective teaching. Teachers who want students to be respectful and receptive need to demonstrate their own respect and receptivity to students. When teachers don't display what they say, the natural authority given to teachers by students, as well as the students' commitment to learning, significantly decreases.

3. Effective teaching requires openness of heart and mind toward students. When teachers are settled and open in heart and mind, information naturally flows to students. When this is not the case, students become disinterested, bored, and more unruly.

4. Knowledge resides deep within each person. The communication skill of teaching involves helping people enliven knowledge within themselves and draw out or express it in action. It first involves helping students get to the stage where they are willing and open to unfold new knowledge. The inward flow of the cycle of feeling, thinking, and behavior in teaching involves settling down students' emotional behavior through skills such as listening and emotion management on the part of the teacher. This is greatly facilitated by reducing stress and increasing inner silence in both teacher and student. Once some level of settled receptivity is achieved in the students, then engage the heart, mind, and behavior in the outward flow of the cycle of feeling, thinking, and behavior. These processes together make up a teaching cycle.

5. On the level of heart, the teaching cycle involves first inspiring students by explaining the usefulness of the knowledge to help them fulfill their own goals. An attention-getting opening that establishes the need, purpose, or practical value of the knowledge from the student's perspective fosters receptivity. Referring back to the practical value of the knowledge occasionally helps maintain receptivity. The heart is more interested in the wholeness of knowledge, and the mind is more interested in analyzing the parts of knowledge. First giving an overall, global summary, syn-

thesis, or wholeness engages the heart, which in turn motivates and energizes the student's mind. Responding to questions with openness, patience, and encouragement empowers students, builds communication channels, and naturally fosters attention and receptivity.

6. Next, engage the level of mind. This involves well-organized, sequential presentations of information analyzing the main points of the general knowledge you are describing. Present a sequence of main points, each explaining a principle that unfolds specific details of the overall idea. Give concrete examples to demonstrate each main or general point.

7. Next, engage the level of behavior. Lots of practice, especially fun practice applying the principles, draws out knowledge from the deep inner levels of heart and mind from within the student into outer behavior. Proceed from inner feelings and abstract thinking to concrete practical examples.

8. The next steps in a teaching cycle include evaluating results through feedback, and enjoying the fulfillment of increased knowledge by celebrating achievements. Feedback involves praise and appreciation that nurtures the deeper feeling level, encouraging openness and inspiring further receptivity. Effective feedback is empowering, focusing on improvement. It is in the form of constructive suggestions to work toward the next level of accuracy and refinement, rather than just pointing out mistakes. Give feedback at the student's level of understanding, clearly expressed, or clearly legible if in writing. At least two positive statements for each somewhat negative or critical one is a helpful guideline in giving feedback, such as in grading.

9. A summary conclusion completes a teaching cycle. The initial need is restated, and how the new knowledge fulfills the need is described, based on the deeper level of understanding and experience the student now has. A teaching cycle thus includes: openness to the student, settling down emotions, mind, and heart; establishing the need and value of the knowledge, a global statement of the knowledge, main points alternating abstract ideas and concrete examples, practical experiences applying the knowledge, empowering evaluations, and an integrating summary.

10. A teaching environment with few distractions helps each student access deeper levels of listening, thinking, and feeling. In addition, presentations that use several sense modalities such as videotapes, pictures, graphs, audio tapes, computer simulations, hands-on exercises, and role-playing practice can help maintain interest and help make abstract ideas more concrete. However, useful information presented with openness, interest, clarity, and a little humor frequently can be sufficient for effective teaching and learning.

Examples of How to Use This Skill

EXAMPLE 1

Ineffective use: Conni decides to get her real estate license. To minimize cost and not be locked into a schedule, she orders a home study course and basically plans to teach herself. As she starts to get into it, she feels a bit overwhelmed by all the details, and she finds it increasingly difficult to talk herself into studying the material. She gets down on herself for not carrying through with her goal, but decides that maybe she isn't very interested in real estate after all. There seems to be a lot of legal detail, there is a low rate of success versus attempts to sell, according to the material. Reasoning based on emotions, she starts to think that the prospect for lots of rejections by people taking time but not actually buying a house seems like it may be too difficult.

Effective use: Six months later, a friend at work expresses some interest in real estate. They decide to study the materials together one night a week after going to the gym and having a light dinner together, and to connect with an old acquaintance who is a real estate broker. The broker is encouraging and gives them a vision of the social nature of the work of meeting lots of people and having fun sharing in the excitement of their search for a new home, as well as helping others sell their home. Conni enjoys the training, passes the tests, and ends up working with the broker.

EXAMPLE 2

Ineffective use: As an outstanding athlete in high school, Randy wants to help his son, Gabe, also become the best quarterback he can possibly be. He has read about the communication skill of teaching, and decides to model his training of his son by it. He makes an outline of stages of training, and also makes a checklist of good and bad form that Gabe is using in practice. The process starts fine, but Gabe seems distracted, and Randy increasingly gets frustrated and annoyed at him. Gabe feels very sensitive about any negative criticism by his father, which it feels his father is doing a lot. At one point, Gabe blurts out that he didn't really want to play quarterback anyway, because it's just too hard for him to do things the exact way his father did it; he doesn't feel like he can live up to his father's standards.

Effective use: Randy recognizes that his son has a lot of natural athletic talent, but also is a sensitive person. He decides that what role he will play as the father in his son's athletic training is a delicate matter. He recognizes that the type of feedback, and especially pointing out mistakes, needs to be done with special attention and care. He has several discussions with his son about sports, explains his view of the pros and cons of the different sports, takes him to several sporting events, and has his son talk to athletes in various sports. He also develops a plan with his son about what role he will take with his son in the training process. His son builds trust that his father will not be disappointed if he doesn't do everything right, and together they begin training in the sports and positions his son wants to try out. Randy carefully and effectively encourages his son at the various stages of the training process, focusing on what he is doing well. It goes really well.

EXAMPLE 3

Ineffective use: Mr. Prague loves physics and tries to convey to his students how exciting it is. He realizes it is a hard subject for many students, but feels he must cover all the text material and has found that the only way is to jump right in. He makes a special point to be available to help students, but only a few ever come. He becomes disappointed that so few students show interest in this fascinating topic. After three years of teaching, he changes jobs.

Effective use: Mr. Prague talks to the principal and agrees to experiment with teaching strategies. They interview students about their interests, how Mr. Prague comes across in class, and where they get stuck with the material. He begins to get better results by starting class with what students are interested in and showing how learning the physics behind it helps students do better, such as in skateboarding, electronic music, soccer, biking, or computers. Mr. Prague realizes that his primary interest has to be the students. He begins to think about how change in his students as they learn can be related to physical processes of change in nature, and gets inspired to work on writing a book about the learning and teaching of physics.

SUMMARY OF CHAPTER 29: Teaching

1. Teaching requires systematically applying communication skills.
2. Being a good role model is fundamental to teaching.
3. Teaching requires openness of heart and mind toward students.
4. Teaching is to help enliven knowledge within being, heart, and mind.
5. Establish the need and value of the knowledge for the student.
6. Alternate abstract ideas with concrete examples to build clarity.
7. Include lots of practical experience to build usefulness of the knowledge.
8. Effective evaluations nurture the fine feeling levels of the student.
9. Apply the new knowledge to the initial need in a concluding summary.
10. Openness, interest, clarity, and humor create teaching effectiveness.

Putting It All Together:
Attending, Engaging, Listening, Emotion Management, and Solution Skills

Key skills to use in establishing assertive balance in yourself include disengaging, grounding, resetting, solution orienting, self-talking, decision making, and asserting.

Key skills to use in helping other people settle down include validating, empathizing, disarming, venting, respecting, and empowering.

Key skills to use in team problem solving include solution orienting, reframing, solution building, asserting, self-disclosing, empowering, and motivating.

There are many layers within each of the levels of behavior, mind, and heart. At times the exchange of thoughts and feelings can be on deep levels of mind and heart, and at other times it may remain on more expressed layers and levels of emotion. With lots of enjoyable practice in the sequential approach described here, there will be more frequent occurrences of deeper communication that is fulfilling for everyone involved. Miscommunication will be greatly reduced, without having to put much attention on it.

SECTION FOUR

COMMUNICATION SKILLS ON THE LEVEL OF HEART AND FEELING

This fourth section of the book primarily deals with the inner level of heart and feeling. This level relates to unobservable, inner feelings that are the basis for the more expressed levels of mind and thinking, and body and behaving. It primarily involves developing goals for behavior and enjoying the results of behavior. It is the level at which healthy communication between people is deeply gratifying—the level of loving connections with others.

Once emotions have settled down through listening and emotion management skills, and also once the mind has settled down with healthy solution building, then the level of heart is enlivened and becomes engaged to bring out deeper and more fulfilling levels of communication. This is the level that is most involved in very uplifting feelings of affection, appreciation, love, devotion, and happiness.

Communication skills on the level of heart and feeling involve comfortable and enjoyable ways to open up and deepen the expression of positive, enriching feelings that bring deeper meaning and joy to our lives.

EMPOWERING SKILLS

Empowering skills are communication skills that help people connect more fully with other people on the level of heart and feelings. They are focused on showing openness in order to encourage openness in other people, and on identifying and drawing out positive deeper feelings of self-respect and love for others. The chapters in this section include the advanced skills of asserting, self-disclosing, respecting, motivating, empowering, mediating, counseling, parenting, and partnering.

CHAPTER 30
ASSERTING

 Asserting refers to expressing goals, plans, and behavior in a balanced manner that demonstrates both self-respect and respect for others.

1. The skill of asserting relates to balanced action. Asserting helps people express goals and plans in cooperation with other peoples' goals and plans. It involves standing up for yourself in a way that respects both yourself and others.[6] Non-assertive behavior is not standing up for yourself, or consistently holding back from expressing goals and plans. Aggressive behavior is acting in a way that intrudes on others. Aggressiveness is not a stronger form of assertiveness, but rather is an unbalanced form of behavior that can be damaging to oneself and others. It may seem necessary in a few situations, such as in life-risking physical struggles, but even then assertive balance is usually best. In simple terms, aggressiveness is associated with being mad, non-assertiveness with sad, and assertiveness with glad. But also aggressiveness and non-assertiveness are frequently fear-based.

2. The skill of asserting involves taking responsibility for your actions. 'I' statements are assertive statements that foster clear, direct, responsible communication. 'I' statements contrast with 'you' statements that externalize responsibility, such as, 'You make me mad,' which can subtly contribute to feelings of powerlessness.

3. Here is a good format for an assertive "I" statement:
   "I feel _____ when (you) _____ because _____."
   For example: "I feel frustrated when the stereo is loud (or you play the stereo loud) because it distracts me from studying;" rather than, "Turn down that stupid music!" "I really laughed at your joke;" rather than, "You make me laugh;" "I'm glad you did that part well because it shows you can do a good job. Let's finish this part too;" rather than, "You didn't get it all done—why?"

4. When making an assertive statement about emotions or feelings, name the emotion or feeling. Instead of saying, "I feel like you may not want me to stay," or, "I feel like you didn't know what I was saying, but I don't know if that's right," be more direct and clear with your statement, such as, "I feel uncertain," or, "I don't know what you want," or, "I feel confused..."

5. Expressing thoughts and feelings in a direct manner at the right time increases your own confidence, as well as respect from others. But asserting yourself rarely works when other people are upset. At that time, postpone expressing your feelings, and assert your skill to help settle things down. When upset, people will mistake even balanced assertive statements as being aggressive.

6. Whenever you choose to postpone expressing your own feelings and thoughts because the timing is not right, however, find opportunities to express them later.

You have the right to decide whether or not to assert yourself. But your choices have consequences. Getting stuck in non-assertiveness blocks the smooth flow of energy, and even can promote aggressiveness toward you by others. Healthy communication involves standing up for your rights and taking opportunities to express your own thoughts and feelings at times other people are able to listen and accept them.

7. Assertive people apply win-win strategies. A good example is in competitive sports. Assertive athletes have performing their best as the goal. This requires balance, and it also results in the highest likelihood of winning. You have control over your actions, not over the results of the actions. Whoever ends up with the best score, it is healthy and productive if competitors have done their best—even though we certainly want to win.

8. An aggressive win-lose focus can undermine performance. It can result in getting over-emotional, wasting energy, losing good judgment, and making costly mistakes. When the only goal is winning, losses can be devastating, interfering with performance and reducing the likelihood of winning. For years, professional baseball players have said, "Stay within yourself." This recognizes that peak performance involves staying balanced and not getting too aggressive or over-excited. By doing your best, chances of winning are improved.

9. Non-assertive people need to practice moving energy locked up in the heart into mind and action. It is helpful first to identify goals and plans, then take small risks to act on them in order to get energy flowing more smoothly. A little venting of anger due to built-up resentment also can sometimes help. Aggressive people need to practice thinking and planning using the mind, and practice observing others. It is also helpful for them to take time to "smell the roses," to appreciate the here-and-now without pushing so hard to change things. These people need to learn to accept themselves more fully and think through more carefully the potential effects of their actions. When assertive balance is the pattern, however, occasionally strong assertive statements can be effective. Assertiveness involves, however, listening carefully first and understanding the situation, before giving your point of view or evaluation about something. Asserting just to look like you are standing up for yourself is not effective unless you are first clear what the issues are and what you are supporting in your assertive expressions.

10. Asserting has many levels, from strong to refined expressions. Asserting in a political convention, classroom, family meeting, or expressing love to your spouse all have their own level of sensitivity. But in each case, the principle applies of settling down strong emotions first, as much as possible, so people can actually hear your assertive statements. In asserting, good timing makes for success. Effective asserting is quite important for avoiding depression and actively creating more happiness.

Examples of How to Use This Skill

EXAMPLE 1

Ineffective use: Melissa loves her husband and couldn't bring herself to leave. But even from the beginning of their relationship she has not been very happy, and now that the children have moved out it is becoming more uncomfortable. She feels her husband is a taker, always expecting things from her, which she usually does. On rare occasion he says or does something nice, but doesn't really engage with her as a partner in living their life together with playfulness and mutual devotion. At times, he is emotionally rude and harsh, but he has little sense or recognition of this behavior. Melissa is spending more time with community projects, but feels less and less like she is in a marriage with her husband, who also seems to be eyeing other women even more than his usual pattern. Melissa wants to do something about it. Her oldest sister says she should move out and go take care of their aging mother. Her other sister says that she needs antidepressants.

Effective use: Melissa realizes she is stuck in a non-assertive pattern of behavior that has weighed her down emotionally for many years. She decides to begin working her way toward more balance. She starts with learning communication skills. She also begins to take morning walks. Slowly she begins to notice a little more energy, and she is more playful around the house, including with her husband. Her husband actually acknowledges her new behavior, and on two occasions this month they have begun talking about their life goals now that the kids are out of the house. To her surprise, she finds that her husband wants to get away from his tedious job and travel for the entire summer next year. They start enjoying getting ready for the extended drive, including buying and refurbishing a used RV. He starts having more fun, and even said he wants to learn how to be more respectful and kind to her.

EXAMPLE 2

Ineffective use: Because Joe is gone on the road all week, he wants to enjoy being with his family on weekends. He doesn't want to have to clash with his teenage boys over their messy rooms, foul language, and general rudeness. He wants just to have a little peace in the family and do all he can to make his kids happy. He feels that the best thing is not to push them, because then he quickly gets angry and blasts them. But these days his sons rarely are around to do anything with him on weekends.

Effective use: Reflecting on his whole family situation, Joe realizes that things have gotten almost out of control, and he and his wife have not worked together for years in how to build unity in the family and work together for effective parenting. He decides to take action. First he will just focus on connecting with his wife, learning about what she wants in her life, and on what is fun for her. On some subtle level, their sons actually begin to notice something different with their parents. They seem to be a little closer to each other, and it is easier to be around them. One evening they all talk together about how it might be fun to start a family business. They all agree for the next month to have dinner together on Sunday afternoons and talk about what kind of business might be interesting and worth trying.

EXAMPLE 3

Ineffective use: Lin grew up in a strong tradition that emphasizes showing respect for other people. But in the country she now lives, she has noticed that people seem to have a different approach. A friend even said she lets people "walk all over her." She decides to start standing up for herself. She says to a co-worker, "I can't stand hamburgers and fries. I like nutritious food that doesn't make me want to fall asleep an hour later. I'm tired of you deciding where we go for lunch all the time." The co-worker says, "You've never said anything about it before, and now you're blaming me? Fine, I'll just go by myself from now on; I'm out of here."

Effective use: Lin asks a co-worker, "A friend said I let people 'walk over me'—do you think so?" The co-worker says, "Well, you're very nice, but you never say what you want. For example, we've been to the same place for lunch, but you've never said anything. Maybe you like other kinds of food, I don't know." Lin says, "I was just trying to be nice. The market café does have more variety." The co-worker says, "If you want, let's try it."

SUMMARY OF CHAPTER 30: Asserting

1. Asserting is standing up for oneself with respect for self and others.
2. Miscommunication is due to non-assertiveness or aggressiveness.
3. "I" statements reflect taking responsibility for one's own emotions.
4. "I feel...when you...because..." is an effective format for asserting.
5. Timing is crucial in asserting yourself effectively.
6. Healthy communication involves being assertive when others can hear.
7. Holding in emotions can result in aggressive outbursts.
8. Assertive people work toward win-win solutions.
9. Peak performance requires maintaining balance, not being aggressive.
10. Healthy asserting involves balance of mind and heart.

CHAPTER 31
SELF-DISCLOSING

 Self-disclosing refers to communicating information about yourself in a manner that fosters openness with other people.

1. People usually like to talk about themselves and want to tell others about their own experiences, accomplishments, interests, knowledge, and opinions. They will frequently reveal information about their lives to a willing and skilled listener. People naturally open up when they are feeling safe and secure, and when willingness to open up is mutual and is appropriate to the situation. This can be fostered by a little bit of talking openly about yourself.

2. The communication skill of self-disclosing involves telling other people information about yourself. This demonstrates that you feel secure and comfortable talking to them. It helps establish an environment of acceptance that is the basis for deeper and more fulfilling communication. It encourages people to open up to you in return. But it needs to be done in a way that is sensitive to the level of interaction and intimacy that fits the situation.

3. Personal information is similar to personal space. It is common to feel uncomfortable when people you don't know are too close physically. It frequently takes time and experience with people to begin feeling comfortable being close to them. In the same way, it takes time and experience with people to become comfortable talking about personal and private information with them. In some cultures, it is easier to be close in physical personal space in public and much more difficult to talk openly.

4. The same pattern of approaching communication with other people from the outer levels of behavior and emotions to the inner levels of thoughts and feelings works with self-disclosing. In general, the communication skill of self-disclosing involves progress through outer levels of information about your life and slowly working toward more private, inner levels of feelings as the comfort level between you and other people increases.

5. Even though our entire being is expressed in every action we take, self-disclosing does not mean putting it all into words and telling others all the private details about our lives. There are degrees of self-disclosing. Initial degrees of self-disclosing may involve asking and answering simple questions related to the immediate outer environment. Examples include talking about circumstances of the moment such as the airplane flight, a book or magazine article being looked at, the traveling you are doing, or possibly general comments about current events in the news or general impressions about literature, TV, or movies. A little more personal might be to talk about your own behavior, such as your line of work or activities you enjoy.

6. A higher degree of self-disclosing might involve discussing your thoughts about something in your present or past life, future plans, or stronger personal opinions or ideas about things both you and the other person know or have heard at least something. A high degree of self-disclosing might involve discussing personal feelings about the challenges you have had in marriage and family, your feelings about yourself, or your immediate feelings about the person with whom you are talking.

7. As a general guideline, disclose a little more information about yourself than what others are disclosing to you, but in the *same range* of privacy and intimacy. Avoid disclosing very personal information when the other person is not reciprocating. It is natural to be more open discussing private information with people you know well and trust, and also to disclose much less private information to people you don't know well. If you are interested in talking about something that is usually private, introduce the idea and ask first whether they are comfortable discussing it with you. For example, you might say, "I realize we don't really know each other; but would it be comfortable talking about a challenge about my work that is on my mind?"

8. On occasion it may be appropriate to disclose personal information publicly to people whom you may not know at all. For example, you might give a special talk at a meeting about how you worked through a family or health crisis. At other times, however, self-disclosure of very private information probably will not be received well. It can contribute to other people feeling uncomfortable and closing up, which can restrict communication. This is especially the case in situations where other people might feel obligated by your self-disclosure to reveal more about themselves than they are prepared to do.

9. A key aspect of fostering deeper communication is to maintain focus on the other people with whom you want to communicate. Talking too much about yourself moves the focus from the other person to yourself, which could result in the person concluding you are not really interested in her or him. On the other hand, starting with an appropriate level of self-disclosure can get the communication process going.

10. Along with building new relationships and deepening continuing ones, a benefit of the communication skill of self-disclosing is that it can help you understand and accept yourself more, such as a pattern of thinking or bias you might have. It also can promote assertive balance and more openness.

Examples of How to Use This Skill

EXAMPLE 1

Ineffective use: When Heather's half-sister-in-law Birgit called and said they were going to be traveling to a national park, would be passing through Heather's city, and would like to visit, Heather was enthusiastic about it. Since it had been 10 years since they were last in contact, they briefly summarized what was going on in their families. After a couple minutes, Birgit said that she wanted to be open to Heather and said Heather's husband was flirtatious the last time they visited, and then asked about whether this was still an issue in their marriage. Feeling a bit surprised and overwhelmed by Birgit's disclosure and questions, Heather lost her enthusiasm, the conversation deteriorated, and it ended with Birgit saying they weren't really sure whether their schedule would allow a visit, and that perhaps they should just call at the point in their trip when they knew how much time they would have.

Effective use: When Birgit heard Heather's enthusiasm about a possible visit, she said she would call again in a week and then they could talk more about it. They have three conversations and build up more trust before Birgit brings up her concern about Heather's husband.

EXAMPLE 2

Ineffective use: While visiting his aunt for the first time in several years, Mr. Coffey is captivated by his aunt's beautiful and interesting teenage daughter, who is, quite to his surprise, very much into reading classical literature, a long-time hobby of his. When he gets a chance to talk to her alone in the den, she asks about his work as a travel magazine editor. Mr. Coffey decides to be a more open toward her. Without any improper intentions but rather just ineffective communication, he begins by telling her that he has never been married, that he lives alone in a nice apartment with a beautiful view of the nearby university grounds, and that he reads a lot to distract himself from feelings of loneliness. During this initial discussion, she quickly starts to feel uneasy and shows some restlessness. After a couple minutes, she says that she remembers she had promised to call a friend this afternoon, and quickly leaves the room.

Effective use: When Mr. Coffey first gets a chance to talk alone with his aunt's daughter, he discloses that, like her, he also enjoys reading classical literature, and would enjoy talking about it when she has the time. She responds by mentioning the name of the book she is now reading. Mr. Coffey tells her that he read the book quite some time ago, and would be interested in hearing what she felt about the book so far. He also said he recalled much of the plot, but asked if she would describe what was currently happening at the point in the book she was now reading. They ended up having a nice conversation, and agreed to continue talking about the book the next day.

EXAMPLE 3

Ineffective use: In his first visit overseas, Marvin wants to make friends with other professors. He is very open and tries to let them quickly know what his life is like, his frustrations of dealing with the unbelievably petty politics of academic life, as well as the challenges he has at home with his wife and stepchildren. He becomes confused when his newly introduced colleagues don't seem to want to talk much about their personal lives, but rather seem to talk only about research and about American TV sitcoms.

Effective use: Marvin decides to ask Gopal, also a college professor and his host for the visit, how to develop friendships with people in Gopal's beautiful country. Gopal explains some of the social traditions in his country and the importance of building trust on a professional level with each other as the means to build more openness on personal levels. Toward the end of his one-month stay, Marvin has connected well with several professors and their families. He plans to continue communicating with them by e-mail after he gets back home, and is considering returning with his entire family.

SUMMARY OF CHAPTER 31: Self-Disclosing

1. People usually like to talk about themselves to a willing listener.
2. Self-disclosing helps other people feel secure talking with you.
3. Treat personal information similar to personal space.
4. Progress from outer to inner levels of personal information.
5. There are degrees of self-disclosing personal and private information.
6. Telling your feelings about family is a high degree of self-disclosing.
7. Self-disclose a little more information than the other person.
8. Avoid pressuring other people to self-disclose.
9. Focus on the other person and don't talk so much about yourself.
10. Self-disclosing helps develop clarity and confidence about yourself.

CHAPTER 32

RESPECTING

 Respecting refers to being accepting, receptive, and courteous to yourself and other people.

1. Respect for others begins with the feelings and thoughts you have about yourself. Accepting your own skills, accomplishments, and areas needing improvement helps develop self-respect, which is the basis for respecting others. This involves not pushing yourself all the time to hurry up and do more. It involves enjoying the current challenges in your life while alertly and systematically asserting yourself to step toward the next progressive level of goals and plans.

2. Respecting yourself and others is fundamental to healthy communication. Like listening before expecting others to listen to you, the way to gain respect is to show it by treating others how you want to be treated. Other people will not be open to hear what you say if you don't first show respect for them.

3. The first step in demonstrating the communication skill of respecting is to show respect by listening to what others are saying. Applying listening skills will help ensure that your respectfulness is presented effectively. Connecting with others through summarizing, validating, and empathizing, as well as with basic attending skills, such as looking at them and not staring or standing too close, are important parts of showing respect.

4. The skill of respecting expresses openness, receptivity, and acceptance of other people in both verbal and non-verbal behavior. This involves listening to other people without making quick judgments about what they happen to look like, how they talk, or what they are doing with their lives. It means avoiding closed, restricted body language or speech that might interfere with other peoples' sense of comfort with you, or even with themselves because of feeling hesitant about how they are coming across and being evaluated.

5. The communication skill of respecting involves having the presence of mind to value others as they are and not demand they be the way you want. It is being able to hear other peoples' ideas and points of view, even if they differ from your own. It means being tolerant of their right to have and express their own thoughts and feelings. It involves avoiding responses that discount, dismiss, or disregard other people. Sometimes this is called to "dis" someone, usually considered to be insulting or *dis*respectful behavior.

6. Respecting involves sensitivity to the subtle feelings underlying communication between people. One example is talking with others, rather than talking *at* or *to* them. Talking to others sometimes conveys a sense that things are one-sided, as if

you're going to tell them something, whether or not you will listen to them. It is a bit more respectful to say, "I would like to talk with you" rather than, "I would like to talk to you;" or, "Let's discuss this;" rather than, "I'm going to tell you about…" Framing communication as a discussion between equals is an important part of respecting. In return, they will show more respect for you and will place more value on what you say.

7. Respecting also involves taking full responsibility to help others become clear about what you're saying. Avoid statements such as, "You're not listening;" or, "Can you understand what I'm saying?" or, "Do you know what I mean?" or, "I don't think you understand." These can result in others feeling that you think they aren't clear or intelligent enough to grasp your meaning.

8. Avoid making statements that suggest other people are wrong if they cannot understand what you are saying. Generally, it is your responsibility to speak in a manner they can understand, not their responsibility to attribute the correct meaning to what you are saying. Instead, show more respect with statements such as, "Am I expressing the meaning clearly?" "Was my response vague?" "Did my comment make much sense?" "Would you tell me what you got from what I said, because I'm not sure I described things as I intended?"

9. Basic courtesy is also an important part of the communication skill of respecting. In addition to speaking in a harsh tone of voice or running on without letting other people talk, which immediately turns other people off, one of the most common discourteous behaviors is to interrupt others when they are talking. A common example is cutting others off with a statement such as, "I know what you mean;" without letting them finish telling you what they actually do mean. Making a point of understanding them before you try to get them to understand you is basic to respecting other people. Except in danger or emergency, abruptly walking away, or turning to talk to someone else without apology, is usually received as quite disrespectful. Also disrespectful is not asking how the other person is doing if you were asked.

10. Communicating with other people is like dancing. It requires attention to avoid "stepping on their feet." Each person has a style of speaking, like a style of dancing. If you listen carefully, you can identify when they are ready to receive input or want help from you to keep the discussion going. Learning when to assert your own comments into a conversation is an important skill for showing respect that takes careful listening and practice. Many people are not particularly skilled in timing properly the dance of communication.

Examples of How to Use This skill

EXAMPLE 1

Ineffective use: Scott's father says that Scott rarely helps around the house, and also is rude to his mother. Scott replies, 'All you do is pick on me; you're never satisfied. Maybe if you started treating me with a little respect, without always trying to make me like you want me to be rather than letting me be who I am, you might get a little more respect from me.' Scott's father says, 'You know, I was never treated well by my parents. They always thought I wasn't smart enough to go to college and learn the fine points about how to communicate, so I'm doing the best I can. I just want you to have it better than I had it.' Scott replies, 'Well, nagging at me all the time isn't cutting it.'

Effective use: When Mike recognizes that things have gotten to be a problem with his son Scott, Mike acknowledges that he may need to learn how to deal with the challenge of parenting a teenager. Although he is not much of a reader, he knows that he can learn new things. He decides to discuss with his wife the possibility of taking a couple seminars on parenting skills, and maybe reading a book with her about it. To demonstrate respect for himself and for his son, he takes responsibility to improve his own communication.

EXAMPLE 2

Ineffective use: When a police car drives up to the house and his son gets out of the car with the police officer, Mike rushes out to talk to his son, Scott, who says that he is being hassled again for skateboarding on the Square. Scott says that the officer is a complete jerk, and his stupid rules are against having any fun at all. Wanting to show support and commitment to his son, Mike says to the officer, 'This is the third time you've nabbed my son, and I'm really getting tired of it. Don't you have better things to do for the tax money the government steals from me for your salary?' The officer says, 'Sir, I'm tired of it too. If you don't know how to control your son, we'll have to arrest him and take him to juvenile detention.' Mike responds, 'Are you threatening us? Big law man, hiding behind your badge. You guys have been on my case all my life, and now your hassling my son, and for nothing. It's ridiculous. It's time for you to start showing a little respect for my family. I'm going to complain to the mayor and city council about this.'

Effective use: When Mike comes up to his son and the police officer, Scott starts criticizing the officer about being busted for having fun. Mike listens to his son, then turns to the officer and says, 'I appreciate you showing the courtesy and respect to bring my son home to me rather than taking him to jail. Do you have a few minutes to talk this through with us? I'd like to get your ideas on how to deal with it. As you might expect, as a parent it's quite frustrating; I don't want my son to get the reputation as a trouble maker.'

EXAMPLE 3

Ineffective use: Amanda is fascinated by a particular religious group's rejection of modern life and is curious about their more basic, quaint lifestyle. When introduced to a group member, she enthusiastically praises the group's courageous message about the ecological brutality of modern society and its greedy self-interest. She asks how she can help the group make people living in the 21st Century understand their bold social experiment. The group member replies that he doesn't know how she could help do this, and that when he wants to know how to do something he asks his parents and other elders first. A bit shocked, Amanda asks why a grown man like him would ask his parents for permission to do anything.

Effective use: Amanda is excited about meeting a member of a particular religious society she has been studying. As she is first introduced to one of the members, she thanks the person for meeting with her. She says that she is interested in knowing more about the group and would like to get permission to talk at length with group members about their approach to life. She then asks if he would guide her on how to do this appropriately, or direct her to the appropriate person to get the information.

SUMMARY OF CHAPTER 32: Respecting

1. Self-respect is the basis for respect of others.
2. Show respect to get respect in return.
3. Use listening and attending skills to show respect.
4. Restricted body language interferes with conveying respect.
5. Respecting involves tolerance for the differences between people.
6. Respecting involves sensitivity to the subtle effects of speech and action.
7. Take full responsibility for helping other people understand you.
8. Avoid suggesting people are wrong if they don't understand.
9. Basic courtesy is an important part of respecting others.
10. Attend to other peoples' signals about the timing of communication.

CHAPTER 33
MOTIVATING

 Motivating refers to inspiring people to take action on healthy goals and plans for higher levels of fulfillment.

1. Basically we humans are simple and easy to understand. By nature we all have the same ultimate goal, and that is simply to be fulfilled. Complexity comes from different ways of understanding how to become fulfilled. If fulfillment is sought outside us in the constantly changing world of concrete things, it is incomplete, fleeting, and leads to craving for more. When it is found inside, it is present wherever we go and is a part of everything we do.

2. As deeper levels of mind and heart are enlivened, understanding about how to be fulfilled matures. Over time the goals that motivate people change, becoming more refined, expanded, and universal. The focus shifts from short-term tangible things such as money and immediate sensory gratification to more abstract respect and appreciation for a job well done. It further progresses to deeper expressions of harmony and love in family and society, and to inner peace and attunement with the natural order in the universe. When people are highly developed in heart and mind, their personal goals are spontaneously more consistent with the welfare of the entire world family.

3. The communication skill of motivating is based on inspiring people. It involves helping people envision a higher sense of purpose for their lives. In part, this is promoted through attention to the level of heart and feeling. People are naturally motivated by getting in touch with their dreams, wishes, desires, and goals. Personal and family goals, as well as vision and mission statements in organizations, are examples of ways to get in touch with feelings and define goals as the basis for increased motivation.

4. Expansion and growth toward higher levels of life are inherently motivating. Attending to this inherent direction of life naturally triggers energy toward higher accomplishment. It is less effective to try to motivate by getting away from a lower level of life, such as avoiding negative punishment. As a general guideline, motivate *toward* rather than *from*.

5. One aspect of motivating is breaking big challenges or goals into small steps or sub-goals that are each achievable. Goals and sub-goals need to be expressed in clear plans of action. It helps further to identify a time schedule for completing plans, and to evaluate and recognize each step of progress.

6. Motivating is greatly enhanced by believing in people, showing trust, asking opinions, sharing decision making, acknowledging contributions, enjoying working together, and treating others as individuals. Listening to suggestions encourages

others to take personal responsibility for team goals. Communication that tends to reduce motivation includes moralizing, blaming, telling people what to do before they want the information, dismissing people's ideas and missing their points, arguing about minor details, sarcasm, making negative comparisons to others, and ultimatums.

7. Giving feedback is an important part of the skill of motivating. It is expressing your own thoughts and feelings about other people's behavior. Feedback that motivates is respectful of others and conveys information that helps people direct their own behavior more effectively. It also demonstrates appreciation, which supports the finer level of feeling in the heart.

8. The core element of effective feedback is complimenting. This involves applying the skill of solution orienting to focus on what was done right and what worked, rather than mistakes. Pointing out positive aspects of behavior supports further attempts to improve; focusing on mistakes can decrease motivation. Giving feedback involves finding something good about what others are trying to do, and making this the primary content of the feedback. It requires observing and listening carefully to identify at least a grain of something positive in other people's performance. It doesn't mean not being honest, or not helping others improve performance. Feedback is best when it is immediate, honest, useful, and supportive. In general, aggressive people feel unsatisfied with compliments, non-assertive people feel undeserving, and assertive people accept them with humility and appreciation.

9. When motivating people who are confident and accomplished, there can be a little more focus on what is still not quite right. Also, using guilt to motivate is more effective when people are doing most things right and have a good sense of responsibility or conscience. Explanations about right and wrong are also more useful in these situations. But if people are beginners or are making lots of mistakes, the most effective focus is on what is being done right. When responsibility and conscience are not developed, guilt and explanation are less effective than immediate behavioral consequences.

10. Giving constructive feedback to other people strengthens their trust in you and respect for your thoughts and feelings. This positive exchange is fostered by the same principle of listening first in order to be heard. Feedback is a two-way street. Actively encouraging and openly receiving feedback from others increases receptivity for the feedback you give to them.

Examples of How to Use This Skill

EXAMPLE 1

Ineffective use: After hearing a talk from a famous motivational speaker, Mark decides he needs to get his life together. He tries to follow the advice of getting clear and specific about his goals. Mark misinterprets what was meant by this, and lays out five goals, the first of which is to have a net worth of at least one million dollars by December 31 of this year, and another goal is to retire by the time he is 35. He thinks the only way to accomplish this is in real estate. He invests $3800 to take a course in it, but finds that after five months he has made only $1000. He starts to lose interest in his goals because he is just not able to find a way to accomplish them. He becomes emotionally exhausted over it, and starts to feel a little down about himself.

Effective use: Mark hears a famous motivational speaker talk about the importance of having goals in his life. He goes up to the speaker after the talk and asks for more detail about what this means, because sometimes goals seem to be inconsistent with each other. For example, Mark explains he has a goal of being financially successful, but he also has a goal of truthfulness and honesty, and he sees that some people who focus on the first goal don't seem to value the second more important goal, which makes having lots of money shallow and meaningless. The speaker thanks Mark for bringing up this very important point about making goals that he has never addressed in his talks. The speaker then begins to recognize some of the differences between goals and clarity of plans consistent with broad-based goals such as honesty. The speaker says he'd like to work with Mark in order develop more refinement in his motivational presentations and training.

EXAMPLE 2

Ineffective use: Jane and her husband, Waylon, discuss parenting of their two grade school children. Jane feels that the kids should be motivated to help around the house just because it is a good thing to do, and should get an allowance every week that is not based on their performance. Waylon thinks that it will be good for the kids to start understanding the relationship between regular work and success. He thinks that allowances should be based on performance, in which the kids earn spending money by contributing to the household and carrying out their chores. As the discussion continues, neither budges at all. But both do admit that punishment made a difference when they were growing up, so they decide to start by at least setting up some clear disciplinary consequences for not doing the chores. Both get busy on other things, and they don't end up talking about it or doing anything about it for the next year.

Effective use: Jane and Waylon recognize that they both have the same general goal of effective parenting and are motivated to implement a better system. But they realize that they have strong differences of opinion about how to motivate their children.

They decide that they will apply their motivation to get parenting training about disciplinary consequences, positive and negative. They agree that their first step is to find out what parenting training is available through the resources in their community.

EXAMPLE 3

Ineffective use: Justin is famous as a dynamic speaker. As the keynote speaker at his old friend's company annual meeting, he describes the trials and tribulations of his rise to success far beyond what he ever imagined. He gives his philosophy of success with examples from the life stories of industry leaders. He encourages everyone to "never doubt, never waste time, and never give in." Afterwards, several employees comment on his enthusiasm and humor. They also happen to make note that his speaker fees equaled the entire annual budget for training of new hourly employees, and wonder whether the cheerleading is really worth it.

Effective use: Ken, the human resource development manager for the company, holds a meeting in which he asks employees about their own personal goals. The discussion evolves into an excellent discussion about how to improve company life. Ken expresses gratitude for the feedback, and everyone agrees to think of ways to implement the ideas. Afterward, several employees comment on how they feel more motivated to work as a team.

SUMMARY OF CHAPTER 33: Motivating

1. Inner fulfillment is present wherever we go and whatever we do.
2. As deeper levels of heart and mind are enlivened, goals mature.
3. Place attention on heart and feelings to help develop goals.
4. Motivate toward positive success rather than away from negativity.
5. Developing achievable plans and sub-goals is important in motivating.
6. Motivation is fostered by believing in and respecting others.
7. Effective feedback supports the underlying level of heart and feelings.
8. Effective feedback involves the skill of solution orienting.
9. For people making lots of mistakes, positive feedback is essential
10. Receive feedback from other people before giving feedback to them.

CHAPTER 34
EMPOWERING

 Empowering refers to fostering self-responsibility and ability to accomplish goals and plans through balanced assertive behavior that results in increased fulfillment.

1. The communication skill of empowering involves locating and bringing out from within people the power to work toward healthy fulfillment of plans and goals. Healthy communicators are able to exchange thoughts and feelings with others in mutually beneficial ways that promote rather than take away the power to control their own lives. They naturally encourage and support others to take responsibility for doing the right thing.

2. High levels of assertive balance, self-respect, self-responsibility, patience, empathy, and ability to observe and listen carefully are required to help other people empower themselves. Self-empowerment is necessary in order to contribute effectively to the empowerment of other people.

3. Empowering involves communicating in a manner that brings out peoples' abilities to build solutions on their own and that reduces feelings, thoughts, and emotions of being inadequate, ignorant, or wrong. It involves avoiding giving advice or trying to offer solutions without first being asked. It includes learning to avoid interrupting, ignoring, criticizing, discounting, or dwelling on minor issues that overlook peoples' assets and ideas.

4. The communication skill of empowering includes connecting with others in a way that goes beyond their limitations to their underlying goodness, and drawing it out with positive encouragement and support. It is based on mature openness and acceptance that guides logic and judgment.

5. Empowering is sometimes thought of as associated with a non-judgmental approach to communication. A non-judgmental approach doesn't mean to disregard judgment or consideration of right and wrong, as if any behavior is as good as any other. It relates to how input or feedback to others about their behavior is expressed. It means to communicate knowledge and opinion in a manner that is respectful of other people and does not undermine their sense of self-respect. In this sense, empowering is quite judgmental, in that there is a strong judgment and bias toward seeing the good in people and encouraging its expression in balanced, assertive behavior.

6. Empowering involves avoiding an authoritarian style when it is not necessary. On occasion, an authoritarian style that involves directly telling people what to do is needed. But more often it interferes with people's attempts to figure things out

for themselves. Patiently supporting people's own decision making, and allowing them to risk mistakes to learn from them, can help empower people to take control of their own lives. It is usually a more effective way of supporting other people than just telling them what to do. However, allowing people to ask and get assistance when it is needed is also empowering, rather than allowing them to get too stuck in repeated mistakes. A balanced assertive approach effectively can empower others.

7. Fostering choice is an important part of empowering. This helps people learn to make and accept responsibility for their own decisions. Helping people identify alternative actions and think through the likely consequences is usually a healthier way to foster self-responsibility than telling them what you think are the right and wrong ways to behave. Pointing out a couple of alternative actions and what the consequences might be, and encouraging others to engage in rational consideration of possibilities, is empowering. Encourage identifying goals first, then thinking through results of plans.

8. Empowering involves effective use of communication skills such as solution orienting, negotiating, and mediating. Sometimes people get stuck in defining an issue or problem. For example, it might be very difficult to get rid of a supervisor or find another job; but the issue may be more easily solved by viewing it as a communication issue that can be resolved through mediation. Even better, perhaps it is solvable simply by settling down and locating within oneself the skills to negotiate assertively with the supervisor.

9. Here's another example. Let's say a young man's car is stuck at an intersection, and you can see he is embarrassed and frustrated about it. It may be *dis-empowering* to say, "Hey! You need to get this car out of the way; you can't park here;" or, "Can't you get your car to run right?" or, "What a bargain your foreign car was, huh!" It would be empowering to say something like, "Let me know if I can help;" or, "May I be of assistance?" If the young man is interested in your help, you might then say, "I'm a mechanic if you'd like some suggestions on checking things out; do you think we need to first move the car to the roadside?"; or, "I'm not a mechanic, but I could help push,"; or, "I have a cell phone to use." These responses offer support while showing respect by not taking over or telling him what to do.

10. The communication skill of empowering is an overall style that involves both uplifting hearts and encouraging responsible minds at the same time. It fosters a stronger sense of self-respect by validating deeper levels of thoughts and feelings. It helps people feel more comfortable within themselves, and helps others work on resolving self-doubts. It requires a healthy, mature balance and integration of heart and mind to empower others effectively.

Examples of How to Use This Skill

EXAMPLE 1

Ineffective use: Wealthy Mr. Coplin decides he wants to help empower less fortunate people in his city. He announces that his company will donate all the donuts that are not sold in his chain of 43 convenience stores to the 17 grade schools in the poorest neighborhoods. He is quite annoyed when he hears that only three schools are interested in his offer.

Effective use: Wanting to help the less fortunate neighborhoods in his city, Mr. Coplin contacts local officials and asks them to advise him on how he might be able to be helpful to the children in their communities. After considerable discussion among the local officials, they give him a list of suggestions, including hiring local teenagers to pick up trash—such as food wrappers, cans, bottles, and cigarette butts—in the neighborhoods surrounding his convenience stores; financing vigorous no smoking campaigns in their neighborhoods; and financing more enforcement of illegal alcohol purchases through his stores. Also on the list is a suggestion to offer in his stores a low cost alternative, healthy snack that doesn't have a lot of sugar, pesticides, and genetically engineered products in it. Mr. Coplin expresses appreciation to the local officials for opening his eyes a bit and empowering him to take more responsibility for the effects of his own businesses.

EXAMPLE 2

Ineffective use: John finally is beginning to understand that his wife, Katrina, is actually quite intelligent even if not very confident in herself. He wants to accept his role to support his wife and to empower her to accomplish more things in her life. He decides that she should get involved in social activities with other women. To help empower her to do this, he signs her up for a year's participation in the most popular women's gym in their community. It's expensive, but he knows she's worth it, and he will help her feel empowered to convince herself that she deserves it. Katrina reacts negatively, and even says it feels like he is always trying to tell her what to do, as if she was incapable. John feels hurt, says that this is a total manipulation of his intentions, and says he is quite frustrated at her.

Effective use: John takes Katrina out for a special dinner, tells her some of the many ways he is thankful for her love and devotion, and asks what he can do to support her own goals. Katrina responds very appreciatively, but says she doesn't really know what her goals are. She agrees to think about it. A week later she says to John that she may like to try out the new program being offered at the women's gym. John says that it sounds like a very good idea, encourages her to check it out, and asks her to let him know how he can help.

EXAMPLE 3

Ineffective use: Coach Ronda tries hard to get her track athletes to excel. She is very straightforward with praise and criticism, according to their performance. Her style is quite demanding, but she is confident she is respected, if at times feared. At least she gets her best athletes to excel, and everyone knows she "loves her girls to death and wants them to succeed." She is finding over time that fewer girls are in track, but more seem to be involved in softball and volleyball.

Effective use: When Coach Ronda asks Coach Eileen about her volleyball teams, Eileen says she first asks each girl what her goals are in playing sports, and then deals with each athlete according to what each one wants out of it. She also tries to avoid criticizing and to focus attention on training in the athlete's next higher level of skill. She has found that the girls seem to feel better about themselves by coaching them using this approach, and that at the same time it has resulted in the girls performing better.

SUMMARY OF CHAPTER 34: Empowering

1. Empowering fosters the sense of power to control one's own life.
2. Self-empowerment is required to help others empower themselves.
3. Empowering helps bring out people's own ability to problem solve.
4. Empowering focuses on the underlying goodness in people.
5. Express judgments in ways that don't undermine people's self-worth.
6. Use an authoritarian style only when it is necessary for the situation.
7. Foster choices to help people develop self-responsibility.
8. An important part of empowering is the skill of solution orienting.
9. Empowering involves providing assistance without being controlling.
10. Empowering requires a high level of balance, a cool mind and a warm heart.

CHAPTER 35
MEDIATING

 Mediating refers to applying healthy communication skills to help other people get to the point where they can resolve their own disagreements and conflicts.

1. Disagreement and conflict unfortunately are common in our lives. All too frequently they are dealt with by non-assertive avoidance resulting in power imbalances and resentment, or aggressive defensiveness resulting in distrust and lack of cooperation. Triangulating, or getting others to take sides, is also frequently involved, which creates misinformation, gossip, and deeper divisions. Often people end up appealing to an authority such as a judge or court to resolve conflicts, which results in giving up power and control over their own lives.

2. An important alternative is the communication skill of mediating. This is a win-win solution strategy in which both parties consider their own and each other's goals and plans in a manner that respects each other. The healthy communication fostered by mediating can transform conflicts into positive experiences of understanding, cooperation, and growth. It is very helpful for many challenges, including family conflicts, neighborhood disagreements, major issues such as custody and other legal disputes, disagreements between employees and employers, and sometimes even disagreements between nations. It promotes self-sufficiency by giving people experience in how to cooperate and build solutions together. In the long-term, the most effective strategy is to develop inner silence and peace deep inside, which has the power naturally to change enmity into friendships and cooperation.

3. The communication skill of mediating involves creating a safe environment that fosters cooperation through the support of a neutral third person not involved in the dispute. The role of the neutral mediator is to establish a comfortable solution space that supports healthy communication. In this setting, people are more capable of connecting with each other and working through their differences to come to mutual agreement. Patience, careful attending, and listening are the keys to successful mediating. The mediator's involvement is as minimal as it can be, allowing the healing process between people to go on its own as much as it can, with both parties taking responsibility to cooperate together. The neutral mediator guides the process when necessary to maintain healthy, constructive communication and avoid the patterns of miscommunication that led to the dispute. Here is a simple format, with the acronym MEDIATE, that fosters assertive solutions:

M *Meet to resolve issue.* Agree on rules with intent to solve issue.

E *Engage in listening.* Listen carefully to other party.

D *Discuss concerns.* Express feelings, privately with mediator if necessary.

I *Identify solution mode.* Build a solution space.

A *Actively listen.* Validate each others' feelings and goals.

T *Team up and think together.* Work together to brainstorm a solution.

E *Embrace agreement.* Accept and sign agreement.

4. **Meet to resolve issue.** The mediator starts by explaining the process of mediating and the mediator's neutral role. Conflicting parties agree to the process, and agree to engage in it with *intent to resolve the issues together.*

5. **Engage in listening.** Each party describes his or her issues and concerns while the other party listens. The mediator may need to manage this process a little in order to maintain a constructive interaction.

6. **Discuss concerns with mediator.** The mediator interacts with each party as needed, separately in private if required, using listening and emotion management skills to help each party express and settle down any negative emotions.

7. **Identify solution mode.** The mediator helps each party create a rational problem-solving mode of functioning—solution space—and gain clarity about their own goals, using listening and emotional management skills as needed.

8. **Actively listen.** The parties express their own thoughts and feelings directly with each other, using listening skills with the mediator's guidance as needed, to build understanding and acceptance. The mediator gets involved only to maintain constructive communication.

9. **Team up.** The parties think together to brainstorm ideas, then narrow them down into a mutually agreed upon solution. Usually easier issues are addressed first to strengthen teamwork. This involves understanding each other's goals, establishing mutual goals, and then working on the means by building plans together to fulfill mutual goals.

10. **Embrace agreement.** Finalize the agreement with all parties signing it, then express appreciation and embrace the process of continuing cooperative relations. If helpful, build into the agreement plans of how to resolve any remaining or future issues. Through this experience, however, frequently people are better equipped and empowered to resolve future issues on their own, without the necessity of a third party.

Examples of How to Use This Skill

EXAMPLE 1

Ineffective use: Denise has been offered a good job as president of a bank 150 miles away and wants her husband, Warner, to move. But he wants to stay where he grew up and continue his consulting business. They hire a mediator who is respectful, kind, and careful to provide a supportive environment without interfering or controlling the healing process. In the second session, there is a huge argument that's really been building for years. Denise says Warner won't give up his job like she did years before because he can't leave his parents. There's no progress and they even begin to question their marriage.

Effective use: After the first session of no progress, the mediator realizes there is more to the story. He meets individually with each of them, allows them to vent unexpressed frustrations and fears about their relationship, and then helps them talk openly about some of the points with each other. As things are talked through and mutual understanding increases, they design together a one-year trial period during which Warner agrees to go back and forth in a way that allows him to continue his business and also spend time with his wife. The short episodes apart give them needed time to reflect, and with it their love grows. After two years, they buy a business in their hometown, which Denise manages very successfully.

EXAMPLE 2

Ineffective use: Although reluctant, Jeff goes along with his wife's desire to build a new home. They have many little differences through the design stage, and frustrations grow. Construction delays and other problems with the house design result in considerable costs beyond original estimates. Jeff thinks the only way to proceed is if his wife, Ruby, expands her part-time job to full-time, which she definitely is against. They decide to meet about the situation with a lawyer they know. The lawyer says that he has dealt with many divorce situations when couples try to build new homes. He says he will try to help them get through it, but his approach is legalistic. The marriage doesn't survive, the house is left incomplete with major financial loss, and Ruby has to take on a full-time job to cover her monthly expenses. Jeff leaves town.

Effective use: Jeff and Ruby decide that they need to talk to a marriage counselor, who uses mediation in his practice. They together go through five sessions, focusing on building the skills to resolve their differences. This also involves very practical communication skills training, which Jeff and Ruby actually work on and practice. They decide together that for the next two years they will not take long vacations or cruises, will focus on enjoying fixing up their new home on weekends, dine out less, and start a home-based business that will allow them to pay the new mortgage. They begin spending more time with each other and working better as a team.

EXAMPLE 3

Ineffective use: Bert becomes increasingly frustrated by his next-door neighbor, Ben, who sometimes yells loudly at people, including Bert's wife, because of his intense political leanings. Also, his teenagers have noisy late night parties, leave garbage around their yard, and also ran over a hedge Bert planted along the alley in his yard. One day Bert finally expresses his frustration to Ben, who initially reacts with his usual outrage, then suggests that they do an informal mediation with one of Ben's friends who is good at that sort of thing. The mediator doesn't really want to do it, and mainly just watches. Both Bert and Ben express their points well, but there is no resolution. Ben says life has its frustrations, and Bert is too uptight about little things. Bert says Ben needs to accept more responsibility for his actions.

Effective use: Bert and Ben go to a neighborhood mediation service. Over the course of three sessions, they come up with a written agreement about what actions will be taken if there is a continuance of any of the problems. Ben agrees to keep the yard cleaner, and also to work on anger management. Bert agrees not to pursue formal complaints regarding any of the past actions that fed his frustration, and to be friendlier and open in a kind way about difficulties before he gets uptight and angry about them.

SUMMARY OF CHAPTER 35: Mediating

1. Use of authority figures to resolve conflicts gives away control.
2. Mediating is an alternative win-win approach that builds cooperation.
3. MEDIATE is a useful format that fosters positive conflict resolution.
4. The first step is establishing rules that foster coming to agreement.
5. The basis for progress is actually to listen openly to the other party.
6. Settling emotions is done with the help of the mediator.
7. The mediator helps clarify goals and build a solution space.
8. The parties actively listen and assert goals and plans with each other.
9. The parties brainstorm together to build a mutual solution.
10. Mediating fosters healthy communication, leading to cooperation.

CHAPTER 36
COUNSELING

 Counseling refers to applying communication skills to help people settle down and locate in themselves how to fulfill their own goals and plans.

1. Counseling is an advanced communication skill that applies several basic skills described in this book while maintaining assertive balance. The word counseling as used here doesn't mean professional therapy. It just means giving support or informal counsel to people you may know and care about in your daily life. Although somewhat similar, professional counseling involves extensive additional training. The communication skill of counseling referred to here mainly involves attending, engaging, listening, emotion management, and solution orienting. These are also key skills used by professionals.

2. For the most part, however, the skill of counseling described here involves simply listening and helping people settle down. Validating, empathizing, and respecting are particularly important. Sometimes it also involves solution orienting, but people often solve things on their own after emotions settle down. Perhaps the single most useful suggestion in informally counseling others is to encourage getting rest, but bring this up only after people have settled down. In our fast-paced society, the inevitable challenges of daily living end up feeling like problems simply due to fatigue. Rest promotes natural healing, improved moods, better judgment, and increased energy to address issues.

3. The communication skill of counseling doesn't involve telling people how to feel, think, or act. Give any suggestions only after people ask you for input and want to hear it. Present suggestions as options people can evaluate on their own. Generally, avoid giving advice that is unasked, telling others what they should and shouldn't feel and think, or telling them what they must do.

4. One of the best ways to be helpful is to remain settled yourself, with calm voice and relaxed posture, and to listen attentively. Sometimes when people get upset, negative energy may get directed toward you. Other peoples' emotions rarely have anything to do with you, and it is important not to allow yourself to get caught up in them. This is especially the case when you serve as the helper for others to vent emotions. Lose balance and you lose the ability to help. If this happens, disengage and find others to help them.

5. When people are quite upset, they can become oversensitive to what is said to them. Comments that ordinarily are balanced and assertive can seem aggressive to them, resulting in people becoming defensive and even more challenging to talk with rationally. An important aspect of the skill of counseling is communicating in a style that avoids reactions, comments, or suggestions that might be taken in the wrong way.

6. People in a non-assertive pattern of behavior usually want to help other people, but frequently take things too personal, get overinvolved, and complicate matters. People who are aggressive try to take advantage of others, which can be damaging to everyone involved.

7. Solution orienting is a part of counseling that facilitates a positive framework. The way people think about an issue affects the emotions involved. When attention is placed on strengths and abilities people have within them, it empowers them. First help emotions settle down through listening and especially validating. Then, if it is appropriate, ask questions about what's going well, what can be changed, doing something different, and goals and plans rather than problems. This doesn't mean helping people fix things, but rather helping them get to the mental space where they can work on things effectively themselves. If people bring the conversation back to problems, then more listening and validating is needed.

8. Keep it simple. It is not helpful to try to facilitate talking about venting of deep feelings, problems from the past, or dealing with traumatic experiences. Leave these areas for professional counselors. Even many professionals question the value of focusing a lot on past problems. It is important not to promote habits that complicate thinking and feeling. This is sometimes called *psychologizing,* and it isn't effective counseling.

9. When talking with others, you may notice examples of negative self-talking. This could include magnifying negatives and minimizing positives, such as exaggerating failures or flaws and discounting successes or good qualities, jumping to negative conclusions without having facts, thinking that things have to be perfect, or putting negative labels on themselves or others. These are usually best dealt with by just listening and not reacting verbally. If it seems appropriate, gently bring up accomplishments and new, positive approaches, but only if it is easy and comfortable for the person to hear.

10. It is important to be alert to the possible value of professional counseling, similar to suggesting a VCR be tested or an ache might be checked out by a doctor. There are many sources of useful information to understand such situations better. Brochures listing warning signs of psychological distress, special hot lines and crisis lines, and Internet websites, for example, can provide directions. It is very important, however, to take seriously threats of self-harm. In this case, the assertive response is to notify professionals who are specifically trained to deal with such situations.

Examples of How to Use This Skill

EXAMPLE 1

Ineffective use: Mayana has read a lot of psychology and astrology books, feels that she is quite intuitive, and loves to help people with their problems. When Rita, a friend of hers, talked to Mayana about a major clash with her husband, Mayana offered to help. Mayana herself has been married three times and is experienced in deteriorating relationships. She points out to her friend some of the signs of incompatibility and ways men reject their spouses. She helps prepare Rita for the painful divorce process.

Effective use: Fran's niece, 20 year-old Stephanie, is exhausted by caring for her child and also going to college. Stephanie appreciates the help her mother gives her, but gets frustrated by her mother pointing out mistakes a lot. Fran invites Stephanie for lunch and a walk around campus, lets her vent frustrations about her mother and about her husband being stationed overseas for the year. Stephanie relaxes after a while, and begins to describe the interesting design course she is taking. Both enjoy the visit. Fran asks Stephanie if she'd like to have lunch together as a routine, and also if it would be helpful for her to baby-sit occasionally to give Stephanie short breaks.

EXAMPLE 2

Ineffective use: Calvin is a very fine lawyer and also has many friends. One of his friends comes up to him at a local sports event. After a while, he brings up a problem he is having with a female colleague at the local university where he teaches, and begins to express considerable frustration about it, feeling strongly that the colleague is being very manipulative and harassing him. Calvin counsels his friend that he may need a cease and desist order. This frightens his friend, and the conversation is changed into how the university football team is doing this year.

Effective use: When a friend of Calvin's begins to ask him for advice at a sports event, Calvin listens awhile. Over the course of the next few minutes, his friend expresses several different emotions about a situation at his work, while they are also watching the game. Eventually they go back to talking about the game. At the end of the conversation, Calvin says to his friend that he'd be happy to have lunch with him this week if he wants to talk more, but he may want to consider having a private consultation with a human resources staff member at the university, which is likely to be a better way to figure out how to handle the developing situation at his job.

EXAMPLE 3

Ineffective use: Ginger is pleased that her boss would open up to her and ask her about how to deal with another worker in the office who the boss is not getting along with too well lately. Although Ginger hadn't noticed any strain in relations between them, she does feel that generally she can see what is going on in a way that other staff may not have the experience to pick up on. When her boss asks her about things that haven't been right in the work area where the person of concern is working, Ginger conveys several interesting tidbits and observations. Two months later, Ginger learns that the boss has brought in a new person to that area, who is single and attractive, and has promoted the new person over others. Ginger now wonders whether her boss had an ulterior motive that she got sucked into, and whether she dealt effectively in giving advice to the boss and answering his questions in the way she did.

Effective use: When Ginger's boss begins asking her how to deal with a particular staff person, she lets him talk awhile. She notices he doesn't seem to be particularly concerned, upset, or involved, even though he says he is asking for her counsel. Ginger asks the boss if he has talked to the person about his concerns directly. The boss says, 'Well, that's kind of hard to do in this situation. Thanks for talking to me about it,' and the conversation ends.

SUMMARY OF CHAPTER 36: Counseling

1. The communication skill of counseling is not professional therapy.
2. Lots of validating, empathizing, and empowering is the key.
3. Counseling doesn't mean telling people how to feel, think, or behave.
4. Lose balance and you lose the ability to be helpful to other people.
5. Counseling requires dealing with oversensitivity in other people.
6. Non-assertive and aggressive people are less effective as counselors.
7. Solution orienting is a positive framework to deal with challenges.
8. Avoid focusing on deep feelings or past traumatic experiences.
9. Deal with negative self-talk primarily by attentively listening.
10. Take seriously any threats of self-harm and notify trained professionals.

CHAPTER 37
PARENTING

 Parenting refers to applying communication skills to help children develop assertive balance in heart and mind to fulfill goals and plans.

1. The communication skill of parenting involves both unconditional love and conditional boundaries, with cool mind and warm heart working together. Unconditional love is expressed in caring for basic needs, and with use of listening, validating, empathizing, respecting, and empowering skills with an open and warm heart. Conditional training of boundaries is expressed in training responsible behavior through asserting, negotiating, decision making, solution orienting, teaching, and leading with a cool mind. This skill also could have been placed in the section on the level of the mind, because parenting involves training in discipline along with expressing love.

2. Children learn a lot by observing their parents. The degree of coordination of heart and mind in each parent affects the children's hearts and minds. If both parents don't demonstrate balance of heart and mind, expressions of love and duty get mixed up. When love and acceptance are made conditional on behavior, it becomes harder to develop self-respect, which can contribute to non-assertiveness. But when any behavior is accepted unconditionally, it is harder to develop self-responsibility, which can contribute to aggressiveness.

3. Children test limits to learn self-sufficiency. Clear guidelines and consequences provide a secure setting for self-sufficiency to develop. This includes positive consequences for good behavior and negative consequences for bad behavior, so children develop a clear sense of the results of their behavior. Consequences need to be implemented consistently. When guidelines and consequences are not clear and consistent, it is more difficult for children to develop balance in heart and mind. It is also more difficult if one parent focuses mostly on love and the other does most of the disciplining.

4. As toddlers mature into children, clear guidelines and consequences appropriately place choices about how to behave into the children's hearts and minds. This helps them build self-respect and self-responsibility. Children choose how to act. Parents identify actions that don't fit guidelines, and implement consequences—with minimal explanation and minimal anger at the time, and then with more explanation in later teaching discussions.

5. Unclear guidelines and consequences are tested more aggressively by children. Discipline becomes complicated and inconsistent. Parents rather than children end up doing the work of deciding about right and wrong behavior, and also end up nagging a lot. Children remain dependent on parental decisions, place more blame on parents, and sometimes try to pit parents against each other. They can

begin to view their parents as untrusting authority figures that try to tell them what to do all the time.

6. Although parents need to have the final word on guidelines and consequences, as children mature it is empowering to negotiate with parents about guidelines and consequences. An excellent way to do this is through regular family meetings. These are great opportunities to schedule family events, learn assertive communication, and foster family solution building. Write down agreements in a family notebook in order to resolve questions about them later, and to document progress to more freedom as self-responsibility grows. Family meetings narrow the generation gap that alienates teenagers and parents. It is easier to set up this family tradition prior to the teen years.

7. In the teen years, role modeling is even more important. Parents need to accept responsibility for their own emotions. Teens can challenge parents much more strongly and find any gaps between what parents say and do. Parents need to maintain their leadership role as parent-child relationships mature, but the style appropriately changes from less authoritarian control to more supportive mentoring. During this time parents need to get involved in their teens' world, without criticizing it. Otherwise, teens create their own world with friends, and try to parent each other without the needed maturity.

8. If the behavior of children gets out of control, it's especially important for parents to maintain balance. Respect and authority are lost if parents give control of their own emotions to the children. The highest skills are needed in order to maintain both unconditional love and conditional boundaries. Disarming, validating, venting, disengaging, calmly repeating guidelines, and family solution building help parents stick to guidelines and consequences.

9. Parents need to choose wisely any battles with children, and avoid major confrontations over minor issues. The overall safety and legality of the household are major and need to be maintained, without feeling intimidated. Help from school guidance, family, and substance abuse counselors as well as law enforcement and social services, may be needed to reestablish order and maintain it in the household.

10. Children are usually quite sensitive to criticism and embarrassment. It is useful to follow the general guideline of two compliments before each correction. This is even more needed when children are being difficult. Also, the overall emotional tone in the home is set primarily by how parents communicate with each other. Loving, respectful communication between parents interacting with each other directly transfers to the children.

Examples of How to Use This Skill

EXAMPLE 1

Ineffective use: Roger and Karen grew up in quite different family environments. Karen feels that the parental role is to be loving and let the kids learn for themselves. Roger sees parenting as helping the kids learn how to function in the world, which requires training in responsible action. Karen isn't comfortable with the sometimes challenging job of disciplining. When discipline issues arise, Roger and Karen argue about how to deal with it. The kids have learned that when this happens, then they can go and play, and the original problem is forgotten in the parent's bickering, so they don't end up getting in trouble. However, they do notice growing frustration between their mom and dad, and sometimes they overhear him say he may have to move out, which contributes to the children feeling unsafe, unprotected, and restless.

Effective use: Roger doesn't want to break up the family, but feels increasingly frustrated at his wife, who is feeling closed emotionally and a little afraid of him. Roger realizes that the main issue is parenting styles. He proposes that together they take parenting skills training. During the course, they learn that both of them have to express both love and active involvement in disciplining. It takes them four months of working together to develop a parenting approach they both feel they can carry out, and over the next year they implement it. Though it is challenging to learn the new habits, there is improvement, their relationship with each other also improves, the household tension is much less, and it is feeling more like healthy family life.

EXAMPLE 2

Ineffective use: Paul and Paula love their children very much and try to treat them equally by spending the same amount on each of them for clothes, holidays, and college savings. They both work at day jobs, so they feel it is important to keep a peaceful, loving atmosphere in the evenings. They have found it a lot easier not to pressure the kids on homework or chores if it seems to reduce the loving atmosphere. However, they have become dismayed by their kids' increasingly disinterested and even rude behavior.

Effective use: Joe and Jo know that training their kids in personal responsibility helps build self-esteem. Joe, a military man, wants things neat and orderly in the home. But he has learned from Jo that parental discipline requires a healthy platform of unconditional love. They agree to regular family outings, to give their children lots of praise and affection, and also to start a tradition of family meetings to talk things over and agree on house rules and consequences. Their kids begin to show more respect.

EXAMPLE 3

Ineffective use: Tori is a single mother of two children, barely getting by financially. Sometimes her mother helps her by baby-sitting, but mostly she does everything herself. She is not trusting of day care programs, based on her own experiences as a child. Tori has attended parenting classes recommended by her social worker. It has helped a little, but she hasn't used the tools in the way her social worker expects. Also, she is sensitive about being evaluated and under threat of her children being removed from the home. Knowing she must control the children, she also recognizes she yells too much to get at least some order in the household.

Effective use: Recognizing she has to make major changes, Tori considers her options. These include even marrying the guy down the street who gets along with the kids but has alcohol problems, asking her mother to move in with her, and having one of the children live with her sister. She decides what she needs is parenting skills, and also to get more sleep. She discusses things with the social worker, who for the first time is impressed by Tori's focus. They arrange for an in-home program for three months of intense parenting training. They also thoroughly evaluate day care centers, and Tori develops the comfort level to try one out for two afternoons a week. For the first month, she checks in on them several times each day. She slowly relaxes a bit, and works on cleaning and going to the store during day care times. As things become organized, she feels better about herself, enrolls in an exercise class at the local park, and decides to study to be a grade school teacher, while also becoming more effective with parenting.

SUMMARY OF CHAPTER 37: Parenting

1. Parenting skills express unconditional love with training of duty.
2. Conditional love and unconditional behavior decrease self-sufficiency.
3. Clear guidelines and consequences provide security for independence.
4. Clear guidelines and consequences develop self-responsibility in children.
5. Children test unclear guidelines and consequences more aggressively.
6. Family meetings include children in guidelines and consequences.
7. Parenting moves from authoritarian control to mentoring with teens.
8. Respect and authority is lost when parents lose control of emotions.
9. Parents must maintain safety and control without intimidation.
10. The emotional tone in the home is set by how parents relate to each other.

CHAPTER 38

PARTNERING

 Partnering refers to applying communication skills in a committed relationship to create deep, open communication that helps fulfill mutual goals and plans.

1. When two people devote themselves to expressing love and responsibility for each other in a permanent relationship, increased personal growth and fulfillment result. Commitment fosters security that allows deeper, more powerful levels of heart to open. Feelings of love soften daily life and bring deeper meaning to it.

2. The bond between two people creates a relationship space or platform. When both express assertive balance, this platform becomes a stable solution space to work through inevitable differences. Building solutions together is the key to a long-term relationship. Problems intensify over time if not resolved through teamwork, with both partners feeling involved, respected and appreciated.

3. Strong negative emotions damage relationships. The communication skill of partnering involves first working on assertive balance. Avoid venting strong negative emotions directly to your partner. Avoid clashes by the use of listening, empathizing, disarming, and validating, and possibly venting with a trusted friend or counselor. When arguments become harsh and emotionally destructive, tape recording them frequently reduces their intensity, or at least helps identify ineffective patterns. As the emotional temperature settles down, focus on mutual goals and plans. Short get-a-ways are excellent times to do this. Then set up regular solution building talks, with an established time-out procedure. As emotions smooth out, love is re-enlivened.

4. The typical pattern in difficult relationships is an aggressive-non-assertive imbalance, or pursue-distance pattern, related to "fight or flight" reactions to danger. One partner becomes more aggressive and the other becomes more non-assertive. These differences initially may attract partners, but later damage relationships. The more aggressive partner becomes jealous, or unsatisfied, or frustrated, pursues more control, or pushes their partner such as by blaming and ignoring. The non-assertive partner pulls back or distances, which draws out more aggressive pursuing in the other partner, resulting in even more distancing in a negative cycle. The aggressive partner begins to doubt he or she is really loved, and feels stuck in a no-win situation of trying harder but seeming to make things worse.

5. The non-assertive partner can become depressed and resentful, questioning if things will ever improve, or even questioning self-worth and self-identity. This partner can feel emotionally intruded upon and cornered on the relationship platform. This can result in more distancing, such as getting over-involved with other family members' lives, especially children. It can also result in energy going out of

the relationship by getting involved with others, who on the surface seem to listen and understand more. This partner may try to take a stand, but frequently does it in aggressive outbursts rather than balanced assertiveness, fighting rather than asserting effectively. On the other hand, the partner may decide to 'take flight' from the relationship. Overreacting by both partners interferes with sincere attempts to improve. The emotional temperature increases, the relationship platform becomes unstable, and commitment bonds weaken.

6. In such relationships, sincere listening to validate feelings is rarely used. There is blaming, angry resentment, sarcasm, avoiding intimacy, and frequently triangulating by sucking other people such as parents, siblings, or even children into the relationship. Mental and physical health can deteriorate due to stress. Self-destructive habits such as substance abuse, breaking marriage vows, and lying make things much worse.

7. It is perhaps more common in relationships for the man to be more aggressive and the woman to be more non-assertive, but sometimes it is the opposite. Also, partners may express the same pattern in and out of the relationship, or different patterns. Even when both people are generally non-assertive, the pursue-distance pattern can develop over time in relationships.

8. Both men and women pull back when hurt. Usually women will talk about it sooner, while men sulk longer and are defensive if pushed. But miscommunication is due more to stress and lack of partnering skills than gender differences. Progress can be made if even one partner works on it. Over time, communication deficits in the other partner become clearer to both partners. When neither works on it, both continue to avoid responsibility for their own emotions. The strategy, 'I'll work on it when my partner does,' prevents progress.

9. In a marriage, nurturing the fine feeling level is crucial. Sincere attention is required to fine-tune communication skills so that this level is protected and nourished. Taking time each day for listening, validating, and empowering greatly simplifies daily life, saves time, and avoids stress. Especially when men do this, marriages improve. It is a small investment that pays big dividends in health and happiness.

10. Marriage can be wonderful for stability, personal growth, and refinement of heart and mind. But it greatly magnifies the power of a relationship, intensifying both positives and negatives. Relationships succeed on the basis of the ability to work honestly as a team on building solutions to inevitable challenges. Potential partners need to take time to identify behavior patterns that arise only over time in the relationship, and then test solution building skills together, before committing to marriage. Marrying just on the basis of some physical feature or level of success or skill frequently creates more stress later on. Honesty and commitment to the lifestyle of devotion to each other, and ability to solve challenges as a partnership are essential for successful marriages.

Examples of How to Use This Skill

EXAMPLE 1

Ineffective use: Larry and Irene fell in love immediately, due to his athletic fame and her social prominence. Over time, Larry wondered if Irene really puts as much into the relationship as he does. Irene goes along with what Larry wants, but rarely feels listened to, and is increasingly uncertain about what she really wants. When she enrolled in art school, he became suspicious of the fun she had with classmates and wanted her to stop school and work to save money. When Irene comes in late one night, Larry initiates a talk. Irene is frightened when he says he will not tolerate Irene continuing to be so cold and aloof from him, and really doesn't comprehend his concern.

Effective use: When Irene runs into an old sorority friend, she follows up on the friend's suggestion to talk to a counselor. She asks Larry to go too, but he says she's the one that needs to change. Irene takes the initiative, begins to understand their relationship pattern, and slowly works on learning how to show more interest in Larry and assert herself around him. Eventually Larry agrees to try collecting antiques together. They begin having fun traveling, studying, and engaging in long talks about history. They uncover deeper levels of love, appreciation for each other, and fun.

EXAMPLE 2

Ineffective use: Germaine and Diana read a book about marriage and begin to understand how he pursues and she distances in the relationship. Germaine discovers that if he is not so pushy, and is more complimenting to his wife, things settle down and life is smoother at home. He adopts this as a strategy and it seems to work. However, the changes are just to get more of what he wants from Diana. He doesn't open up on deeper levels of feeling with her. He acts nicer on the surface, but in fact is even less committed to the relationship. Now that things are smoother on the surface of the marriage, he can go back to pursuing his interest in finding other women for more excitement in his life.

Effective use: Germaine and Diana realize that the degree of integrity they show to each other will directly affect development of integrity in their kids. They read a book about marriage, feel that it helps a little, but that much more is needed for their marriage to hold together during the more stressful times, when both of them tend to pull back from each other—Germaine into his work and Diana into spending more time with her mother and sisters. They decide to take a weekend every three months to go away and be together with no one else around, for the purpose of having more fun together, as well as talking about their goals, how to accomplish them, and how to become more honest, open, and emotionally intimate with each other.

EXAMPLE 3

Ineffective use: Brothers Larry and Harry decide they will start a business together. Larry is more oriented to administration and finance, and Harry is more oriented to sales and marketing, so they see it as a perfect complement of skills. However, Larry feels a little suspicious of Harry, who is more wild and free with his behavior, including with his memory of facts. On the other hand, Harry has long felt Larry is a bit stodgy and even could be so tight as to restrict the growth of the business. Over time these differences start to show up more, as they get involved with their respective personnel in the business. When the economy takes a dive and things becomes tense, the differences grow into more suspicions, they accuse each other of undermining the business, and they end up fighting over it in court.

Effective use: When Harry and Larry decide to go into business together, they first openly discuss their differences and try to build into the business safeguards to ensure their mutual trust. Both agree to a thorough annual review by an independent auditor, even though it is expensive. Both agree to hire key personnel together, both agree to complete transparency of records, and both agree to review together detailed budgets, expenditures, and contracts. If there starts to be intense tension and insecurity between them, they both agree to sell the business and split the profits equally. As they go along, the business grows and also their trust as they both honor the agreements they made with each other.

SUMMARY OF CHAPTER 38: Partnering

1. Commitment fosters security and deepens relationships.
2. Solution building as a team is the key to long-term healthy relationships.
3. Aggressive-non-assertive imbalances are common in difficult relationships.
4. In difficult relationships, one partner pursues and the other distances.
5. Difficult relationships are due to stress and lack of partnering skill.
6. Males tend to be more aggressive than females, but it can be the opposite.
7. One partner can create progress toward a healthy relationship.
8. First work on developing assertive balance in yourself.
9. A few minutes a day of validating your partner is an excellent investment.
10. Observe patterns and test out team solution building before marriage.

Putting It All Together:

Attending, Engaging, Listening, Emotion Management, Solution, and Empowering Skills

Effective, healthy communication involves expressing feelings and thoughts in a smooth outward and inward flow through heart, mind, body, and behavior.

In the outward flow, express your own feelings and thoughts by first being clear about the goals of your heart, letting your mind decide on clear plans to guide actions considering both short-term and long-term effects, and then acting on the plans with assertive balance. Express them at the time that people are settled enough to hear them. If you start to lose balance, disengage, ground yourself, and then re-engage later, systematically progressing toward your own goals through healthy, well-planned, and well-timed action that fits the circumstances and that respects the goals of other people. When you express your mind's thoughts in the context of positive, respectful feelings from your heart, then your communication naturally will have a healthy effect on others and will be received constructively.

In the inward flow, help other people express their feelings and thoughts by attending and listening carefully, allowing them to express and settle down emotions. Then work with them in solution building and empowering to assert their goals and plans in healthy mutual cooperation with you.

Communicating in this way systematically helps integrate heart and mind. It results in communication that has a healthy, therapeutic influence, naturally and progressively unlocking and opening deeper levels of mind and heart. Importantly, it both protects and enlivens the fine feeling level of the heart and energizes the mind for responsible action that leads to higher degrees of accomplishment, fulfillment, appreciation, joy, and mutual love.

SECTION FIVE

COMMUNICATION SKILLS ON THE LEVEL OF SOUL AND BEING

This fifth section of the book deals with the level of soul and being. This level is the deepest, most subtle level of individual life, deeper than the level of feeling. This level integrates the other levels of feeling, thinking, body, and behaving.

Once listening and emotion management skills have settled down emotions, and solution skills have resulted in practical progress on resolving issues, a deeper connection of mutual respect and love is created that greatly enriches communication. We become more at ease with ourselves and with each other. We are open to exchanging thoughts and feelings on the deeper levels of life, at the very core of our individual being and personality. It is at the deepest level that communication is the most beneficial and fulfilling.

Communication skills that primarily deal with the level of soul and being help people become more integrated within themselves, and help them connect with the wholeness and oneness of life that fully unites all individual selves at their basis. Included in this section are the most all-encompassing skills of integrating and unifying, here called actualizing skills.

ACTUALIZING SKILLS

This final section of this book relates to the deepest and most profound levels of communication. The skills in this category connect the levels within the individual self to each other, and also expand the individual self to connect with the underlying universal level of life.

The communication skill of integrating focuses on improving coordination between the levels of the individual self or personality—body, mind, heart, and ego. It involves listening to and connecting with the deep levels of our own inner nature. It is associated with openness within oneself that is the basis for openness with others. The entire personality reflects more smoothness and inner balance that allows deeper levels of feelings and thoughts to be expressed and exchanged with other people.

The skill of integrating connects and coordinates the levels of behavior, thinking, and feelings within the individual. The skill of unifying goes beyond to connect the individual with the underlying universal basis of life. Unifying actualizes the most comprehensive and fulfilling level of communication, not only fostering deep appreciation and love but also attuning individual life to the universal harmony that exists throughout the universe. It involves listening to the deepest level of our own inner nature. It is at that level that our own nature unites with the nature of the universe, our universal nature, our universal Self. It is at this level that Nature whispers to us her most wonderful secrets.

CHAPTER 39
INTEGRATING

 Integrating refers to fostering healthy coordination of heart, mind, body and behavior for more open and deeper communication.

1. Each individual human being experiences life as a wholeness of experience. The different activities on the levels of behavior, body, mind, and heart all collect together into the experience of who we are as individuals. The experiencer of individual life is sometimes called the *ego*. This level puts together all the feelings, thoughts, and sense perceptions coming from the body and the environment. It is the inner sense of "I," as in "I am." Individual behavior is based in thinking, thinking is based in feeling, and feeling is based in ego or being. The senses, mind, heart, and ego or "I" sense, taken together, make up what is sometimes called the individual self or soul.

2. When the levels of the individual self communicate well with each other and energy flows smoothly through them, the inner strength of ego called *integrity* develops. This meaning of ego does not refer to people being egotistical, which is an immature, aggressive style of behavior, but rather of being a complete, mature individual self. Integrating emphasizes the mature qualities of self-sufficiency, self-respect, and self-responsibility.

3. Integrity is expressed in communication signals that accurately reflect inner feelings and thoughts. Verbal and non-verbal messages fit together and don't give mixed signals. Gestures, facial expressions, voice, and speech are naturally congruent. There is little hiding or disguising of inner thoughts and feelings, plans and goals. People who say they are happy look happy and do happy things. People who say they love you actually act in ways that uplift and support your heart and mind. There is genuine openness and appreciation.

4. The communication skill of integrating involves building integrity in the individual self or soul. An important way to develop this skill is to keep ego, heart, mind, and behavior aligned or consistent with each other. This means that feelings, thoughts, speech, and action—who you are and what you feel, think, say, and do—all express the same thing. It is associated with the courage to be honest and to tell the truth, having "backbone," and "walking the talk." It is being balanced and straightforward, with open, warm heart and open, cool mind.

5. Integrating involves coordination of heart and mind, expressing responsible action with love for self and others. It requires clarity about goals, what you want to be and do. It involves evaluating goals in terms of your duty, and planning that is consistent with responsible goals. It involves openness to feedback to understand the effects of your actions in order to develop higher levels of ethical and moral behavior.

6. Feeling and thinking one thing but saying something else, or saying one thing but doing something else, weakens coordination between levels of the individual self. They have a *dis-integrating* effect, producing stress in the mind-body system which disrupts the flow of energy through feelings and thoughts into behavior. This further clouds the purity and strength of ego, heart, and mind, increasing inner noise and preventing deep communication.

7. Miscommunication within oneself results in miscommunication between people. Intended miscommunication or dishonesty is a passive-aggressive pattern. It breeds confusion, frustration, mistrust, conflict, and more dishonesty in a downward spiral, making life much more complicated. This results in behavior based on more superficial levels of heart and mind. The deeper, more fulfilling levels become hidden, so other people see only the more superficial levels. Intelligent, talented people who manipulate others in this way for their own personal benefit are not integrated on deeper levels of mind, heart, and ego. If these individuals are placed in public leadership roles, they damage the health of society. These individuals need to disengage from public life, greatly simplify their lives, get deep rest, and work on building integrity and inner silence, before taking on leadership roles.

8. Integrity, honesty, and openness don't mean putting into words every feeling and thought you have regardless of their influence. It doesn't mean giving up good planning and judgment in communicating. Not speaking, rather than speaking destructively, is often best. However, the skill of integrating simplifies and smoothes communication. It becomes more natural and spontaneous with reduced inner noise, as well as with practice listening to others and asserting yourself when others have ears to hear you.

9. By effectively using the skill of integrating, others react positively. This fosters trust and acceptance, which reduces confusion and doubt about intentions. Less energy is wasted on trying to manipulate words and body language to make things sound or look natural, rather than being natural and genuine. The skill of integrating reduces the likelihood that people will have non-assertive or aggressive reactions to you, which makes communication much easier.

10. With the skill of integrity, healthy positive qualities predominate in inner and outer life. The goodness that exists in the depth of every individual soul is more expressed. Goals, plans, and actions have more positive effects throughout society. Over time, integrity is much more powerful than money and fame for creating health, happiness, and fulfillment in our lives.

Examples of How to Use This Skill

EXAMPLE 1

Ineffective use: Al has a family history of success in politics, a consistent voting record, and a good reputation. He is offered a chance for a prominent cabinet position if he supports a popular candidate he suspects might have a history of political corruption. He won't have to change any of his policy positions, and he is reminded that this is how the game has been played for years. He decides to go for it so he can serve his country better.

Effective use: When the popular candidate's history is about to come out, Al is asked by his party chairperson to communicate his trust in the candidate in a public statement in order to help 'spin down' the rumors. Al rests for a week, talks at length with his wife about what's important to them and the kids, and reads his grandfather's memoirs and favorite scriptures. He becomes clear that honesty is the best way to serve country and family in this situation.

EXAMPLE 2

Ineffective use: Cheryl has been told by her therapist that she needs to be more true to herself, and to actively assert herself and express what she really feels to the important people in her life, especially her family and husband. Cheryl takes her therapist's words to heart and tries to implement them. When her husband questions her choice of outfits for an important social event for his company, Cheryl feels the impulse to express openly and straightforwardly to him feelings she has held back about his lack of relationship skills, and how he makes her feel like a second class citizen at social events. Her husband gets angry, feels insulted and attacked, and goes to the event alone.

Effective use: When sitting with her husband on the porch watching the sailboats on the lake, Cheryl's husband asks if she enjoyed the party they went to last Friday evening. Cheryl mentions that it was interesting to meet the new staff at his company. She also says that she wanted to talk to him about other feelings she has. When she asks if this is a good time to talk more about it, her husband says and acts like he is open to hear more. She begins by saying, "One thing I want to say is that I feel frustrated about you walking away during the parties and rarely involving me in your conversations with people." After discussing this point awhile in a constructive way with her husband, she also openly discusses her discomfort with how one of the salesmen looks at her and jokes with her. They have healthy, effective communication about issues Cheryl has wanted to discuss for a long time, and they agree to talk further the next weekend.

EXAMPLE 3

Ineffective use: Kory is the owner of a construction company that has 19 full-time staff in the home office. Because he is away from the office on the job site much of the time, he needs to rely on information from supervisors who remain in the office. Christina, the bookkeeping staff supervisor, has been having back problems, for which she is taking pain medications. She doesn't want to disclose her health condition to her boss. But the pain medication does affect her moods, which influences her perspectives about things in the office. Christina expresses concerns about several of her staff. Kory decides to have a staff meeting and to bring up the issues Christina mentioned, but in a general way without naming names or where the information came from. The staff get angry in the meeting, feel falsely criticized, and two people decide to quit.

Effective use: As Kory is talking with Christina about how things are going in the office, he notices that something might be a little different in her behavior. It seems to Kory that what she is saying isn't quite congruent with her body posture and overall emotional expressions. Kory thinks about setting up a staff meeting to discuss the issues in a general way, but first decides to talk more with Christina to get more detailed information about what she is reporting to him, and also to ask other staff members. He finds that Christina's perspective is only part of the picture. As he discusses things more with her, she begins to describe a little more what is going on with her health. Christina has a good work record and Kory values her contributions. He inquires a bit further, finds she is also having some financial problems due to helping her daughter's child who is chronically ill. Kory gives Christina time off to rest, and also pays for some treatments to help her back.

SUMMARY OF CHAPTER 39: Integrating

1. The senses, mind, heart, and ego make up the individual self or soul.
2. When these levels coordinate well with each other, integrity develops.
3. Integrity is when actions accurately reflect thoughts and feelings.
4. Integrity is when what you feel, think, say, and do is consistent.
5. Integrity is developed through clarifying goals, plans, and behavior.
6. Inconsistent feelings, thoughts, and actions produce stress.
7. With lack of integrity, action is based on shallow levels of heart and mind.
8. Integrity and honesty do not mean saying everything you feel or think.
9. Integrity fosters trust and acceptance that simplifies communication.
10. Healthy, positive qualities naturally predominate with integrity.

CHAPTER 40
UNIFYING

 Unifying refers to connecting the individual soul or being with the underlying universal level of life, the universal Soul or Being.

1. We all have some belief, hope, or even deeper sense that we are connected with this vast and wonderful universe on a very deep level. Progress in modern science in the 20th Century has led to an understanding of how the entire universe actually is unified at its deepest level. That has been the message of the wise throughout history, and it is no longer just on the level of hope and belief.

2. Modern science has uncovered increasing unity at deeper levels of nature. As deeper levels have been probed, from cells to molecules, chemicals, atoms, and sub-atomic particles to unbounded fields of energy, we have discovered that everything in nature is made of the same thing. Every piece of this universe is now being recognized to come from a single *unified field* that is the source and essence of everything that exists. This universe, this galaxy, this solar system, this planet, this building, this room, this book, these eyes, this brain, this body, this mind, this heart, this ego, and this consciousness are ultimately the same thing—the unified field of nature.

3. The communication skill of unifying fosters a deep connection with the underlying unity of all of nature. It involves refining behavior, thoughts, and feelings to experience subtler, more integrated, holistic values of life, and directly experiencing the universal basis of our individual and collective life.

4. On the levels of mind and behavior, unifying involves listening and thinking deeply or contemplating how all levels of life are unified. As we gain understanding that all things are connected and that our actions influence everything, decision making develops a broader, longer-term perspective. Our sense of duty and responsibility naturally include not only our individual selves but also family, friends, community, state, nation, and the whole world family. When our actions reflect this broader perspective, it has a balancing, integrating effect that enriches the levels of communication.

5. On the even deeper level of heart, unifying involves deepening our appreciation for the beauty and harmony of life. When we feel devotion, such as in heartfelt prayer, for the creation and the totality of all nature, or for its almighty creator—however personally or impersonally we like to think of it—and are awe-inspired by the infinite eternity of the universe, an appreciation of oneness is enlivened and the bond between all of us is strengthened. The differences that make each of us unique don't overshadow the underlying sameness that unifies us.

6. Appreciating these deeper, unifying levels of nature places the meaning of our daily lives into a more universal context of love and respect for the totality of life. Integrity grows as we recognize the larger context of life we all share, and appreciate more deeply our responsibility in it. Goals, plans, and actions become more all-inclusive and holistic.

7. The skill of unifying not only involves these experiences on the levels of behavior, mind, and heart within the individual self or soul. It also involves going beyond our individuality. Oneness is developed by the direct experience of oneness or unity, not by just partial experiences on the levels of feeling, thinking, and behavior. A completely unifying experience occurs when behavior, thinking, feeling, and individual being are gone beyond, are transcended. This is the most profound form of unifying, in which the individual self directly contacts the unified field. In this direct experience, the mind transcends individual boundaries to contact directly its universal basis, like an individual wave settling back into the unbounded, universal ocean.

8. Action is based in thinking, thinking is based in feeling, feeling is based in ego or individual being, and individual being is based in universal Being. Transcending these levels involves naturally settling down through the levels to their underlying universal basis. This experience is accompanied by deep inner silence and rest, which eliminates deep-rooted stress. In this way, inner noise decreases, allowing the underlying unity of life to be further enlivened in us. Because the unified field is the basis of everything, direct experience of it brings us into harmony with the totality of nature. This integrates heart and mind, fostering spontaneous right action in tune with all the laws of nature.[7]

9. Settling down through deeper levels to the basis of our individual self is the one experience that simultaneously develops all levels of communication. It is direct communication with the source of the entire universe—the unified field. It bridges the gaps that separate us by connecting our individual being to the unified source of all beings—our universal Being.[7]

10. It is fortunate that effective means to develop unifying experiences are now available. If you aren't having that deep experience, the Transcendental Meditation technique is a systematic, scientifically validated personal development technique that facilitates it naturally and effortlessly.[8] Direct experience of the unified field is the ultimate means for promoting healthy, effective communication. With regular experiences of unity, and unfolding communication skills from within, you will naturally develop communication that greatly benefits yourself and our entire world family simultaneously.

Examples of How to Use This Skill

EXAMPLE 1

Ineffective use: When Jared goes to college, he is exposed to a much higher degree of personal freedom and a much wider range of lifestyles than he grew up with at home. He begins to see that he can do just about anything he wants. He is told by his sociology professor that everything is relative, and that nature is fundamentally random and purposeless. He gets into partying heavily, and no longer feels obligated to be straightforward, truthful, or anything else, because none of his new acquaintances are either, and ultimately there is no fundamental meaning to life anyway.

Effective use: Jared understands that being open-minded, accepting, and non-judgmental toward others doesn't mean abandoning rationality and good judgment. He notices a few of his new acquaintances are more together in this way. They are more integrated and clear, and can be counted on to be honest and true as friends. It makes sense to him that how he lives his daily life has an effect on his health, clarity of mind, and ability to accomplish the things he wants. He understands that freedom and responsibility go together in balanced individuals who have a positive effect in the world.

EXAMPLE 2

Ineffective use: Alan has come to appreciate that we are all one big family, and that the boundaries and limitations we impose on ourselves are artificial. He no longer feels we should limit ourselves to antiquated traditions such as marriage. He takes the notion of universal love literally. But he also is finding that the girlfriends he has had seem to have a somewhat different view when deeper relationships are considered. His relationships have become volatile and have produced bitter anger and sadness. Even sociopolitical discussions and dialogues with classmates have become anger-filled and quite destructive. Alan has gotten into a cycle of increasing stress, unhappiness, and irresponsibility, and can't find his way out of it.

Effective use: As Alan grows in his love and acceptance of all people, he also is growing in his sense of personal responsibility and duty. He understands that he can have a deep sense of love for everyone, but also at the same time maintain a deep sense of honor, honesty, and respect for traditions and obligations. He knows that it is appropriate and healthy to express his love and acceptance in different ways in different relationships, such as parents, wife, children, friends, neighbors, and co-workers. He is learning that in daily life it is natural to have unconditional love and conditional, responsible behavior at the same time. He is learning how to unify these sometimes inconsistent tendencies in himself to establish more personal integrity.

EXAMPLE 3

Ineffective use: Serena is deeply convinced that love is really all that's important in life. She sees herself as a free spirit, randomly spreading joy wherever she can. She says she has "been there, done that," and knows that life is just what it is, and the only real harm is in judging things. To religious and spiritual questions, her one message is to just follow your heart and not get uptight about anything.

Effective use: While enjoying a beautiful ocean view with her sister, Serena is drawn to the voices of a passing group, sensing a lively silence in them she has noticed in a few people from time to time. She asks and finds out they are a group of long-time meditators. Serena has learned a lot about life in her 40 years, but also knows she doesn't really have the profound and permanent experience of the wholeness and underlying unity of life that she believes is possible. Over the years she has heard some positive comments about the spiritual value of things such as meditation, but has never practiced them regularly, and the few attempts she made based on things she ran across in books didn't seem to get anywhere. She starts to think that there may be ways to grow inside she has overlooked, and is again open to investigate it further.

SUMMARY OF CHAPTER 40: Unifying

1. The unified field is the source and essence of everything that exists.
2. Unifying fosters a deeper connection with the unified field of nature.
3. Unifying involves understanding how all levels of life are connected.
4. Unifying involves appreciating the beauty and harmony in nature.
5. Unifying allows us to expand and connect more deeply with others.
6. Unifying goes beyond or transcends the boundaries of individuality.
7. Transcending results in deep rest that eliminates deep-rooted stress.
8. The universe is connected to us at the deepest level of our being.
9. Transcending is a direct means to communicate with the unified field.
10. Direct experience of the unified field unfolds all levels of communication.

Putting It All Together:

Summary and Conclusion

The purpose of this book is to unfold healthy and effective communication skills in tune with the natural flow of energy that integrates and unifies our lives. This unique, systematic approach to communication provides a practical and profound way to foster the open exchange of thoughts and feelings that helps achieve our mind's plans and fulfill our heart's goals, building deeper appreciation and connection in our personal families as well as our world family.

To again summarize the overall system of communication in this book, foster peoples' attempts to communicate with you by first carefully listening. Attend from outer to inner levels. Start by attending to body language, then emotional behavior, then the level of mind and thinking, and then the level of heart and feeling. When body and emotions settle down, the rational mind can build solutions more effectively. When the mind relaxes with successful solutions, the heart opens up for deeper, more loving communication.

Once you have listened, understood and accepted other peoples' thoughts and feelings, and the people you are communicating with are settled and receptive to you, then assert your own feelings and thoughts. Express yourself from inner to outer levels. Start from the integrity of your ego, and express your heart's goals and mind's plans in consistent, congruent speech and action, naturally letting the content and logic of your mind ride on a wave of love from your heart.

These healthy communication skills foster assertive balance by refining heart, mind, and behavior. Naturally we listen with a warm, open heart and speak with a cool, responsible mind. Our loving hearts and dutiful minds can then guide responsible behavior that benefits both ourselves and others.

The way to develop these skills is to strengthen communication signals and to reduce noise in the mind-body system. The way to strengthen communication signals is to practice regularly and comfortably the skills presented in this book. Reduce noise in the mind-body system through grounding and deep rest. As inner noise is reduced, each of the levels of ego, heart, mind, body, and behavior are experienced more clearly and are enlivened to be used more effectively in everyday life. Eventually the spontaneous working of all these levels to produce behavior in accord with nature is fully appreciated.

The deepest rest, the most grounded state, comes from direct experience of the ground of Being, the unified field of nature. It is the universal ocean of life that makes up every individual wave of life, the essential core of our individual selves. It is always available

Actualizing Skills

by settling down emotions, thinking, and feeling and then transcending our individual self or being. Unifying individual being with universal Being is the most powerful communication skill. It is really putting it all together—you, me, and everyone and everything in the universe. This is the total value of listening and communicating.

Again, here is the simple chart with which we started this book. Added to it are all the categories of the levels of communication described in this book. It includes the primary functions of each level, the main focus of each level, and the communication skills that generally relate to each level. It ties together all the training material in this entire book.

Let's enjoy the benefits of healthy communication by practicing together these skills on the levels of body and behaving, mind and thinking, heart and feeling, and soul and Being.

Levels of the Individual and Corresponding Communication Skills

Levels of the Individual			Inward/Outward Cycle		Communication Skills
Outer/ Objective	behavior	behaving	action	results of action	Attending Skills
					Engaging Skills
	body		↑	↓	Listening Skills
					Emotion Management Skills
	senses	sensing			
Inner/ Subjective	mind	thinking	plan	evaluation	Solution Skills
	heart	feeling	goal	fulfillment	Empowering Skills
	individual self/ ego	being	I (have) ↑	sense of self ↓	Actualizing Skills
	universal Self	Being			

LIST OF COMMUNICATION SKILLS

(Chapter headings)

1. *Feelings, Thoughts, and Behavior* are the building blocks of communication.

2. *The Cycle of Feelings, Thoughts, and Behavior* involves goals, plans, actions, evaluation of results, and degrees of fulfillment.

3. *Increasing the Positive Influence of Feelings, Thoughts, and Behavior* refers to working with body, mind, and heart in sequence to reduce stress and open up deeper communication.

4. *The Flow of Feelings, Thoughts, and Behavior* refers to how life energy is expressed through the levels of heart, mind, and behavior.

5. *Attending to Gestures* refers to observing non-verbal behaviors, sometimes called body language, as indicators of thoughts and feelings.

6. *Attending to Facial Expressions* refers to observing patterns of relaxed and tense muscles in the face as indicators of thoughts and feelings.

7. *Attending to Voice* refers to listening to voice tone, volume, rate, and style as indicators of thoughts and feelings.

8. *Attending to Speech* to speech refers to listening to specific words and phrases as indicators of thoughts and feelings.

9. *Listening* refers to openly using senses, mind, and heart to receive what other people are saying without distraction.

10. *Prompting* refers to applying verbal and non-verbal behaviors that encourage people to communicate.

11. *Questioning* refers to getting more information or clarifying the meaning of what other people are saying by asking about it.

12. *Matching* refers to listening to key words or phrases other people are using and then using the same words or language context in the conversation.

13. *Summarizing* refers to restating briefly in your own words what other people have just expressed to you, without changing the meaning.

14. *Validating* refers to identifying emotions, naming them, and accepting and encouraging their healthy expression.

15. ***Empathizing*** refers to expressing acceptance, appreciation, and support for what other people are experiencing in their lives at the moment.

16. ***Disarming*** refers to managing the flow of energy to dissipate verbal attacks by expressing acceptance or agreement rather than opposing the attack.

17. ***Disengaging*** refers to managing the timing of communication in order to maintain balance and avoid harmful miscommunication.

18. ***Venting*** refers to managing the expression of strong emotions such as aggressive anger in order to avoid destructive miscommunication.

19. ***Grounding*** refers to resting and then attending to body, mind, and heart in order to re-establish assertive balance and a smoother flow of life energy.

20. ***Resetting*** refers to managing negative emotional reactions by quickly interrupting their development and re-establishing more clarity about goals and plans.

21. ***Solution Orienting*** refers to attending to strengths, resources, and skills that support progress toward solutions, rather than focusing on problems.

22. ***Self-Talking*** refers to communicating with oneself in a manner that supports healthy, positive, assertive thinking and minimizes negative thinking.

23. ***Reframing*** refers to changing a limiting viewpoint and developing a more positive and constructive alternative in order to foster progress toward goals.

24. ***Decision Making*** refers to coordinating goals of the heart and requirements of the environment to plan behaviors that result in increased fulfillment.

25. ***Solution Building*** refers to systematically settling emotions, clarifying goals, deciding on and implementing a plan, and evaluating the results.

26. ***Negotiating*** refers to communicating cooperatively with people to build agreements that are mutually beneficial and that increase trust.

27. ***Presenting*** refers to communicating thoughts and feelings to groups of people in a manner that promotes understanding and acceptance.

28. ***Leading*** refers to inspiring and guiding people to work toward achievement of healthy goals and plans that result in increased mutual fulfillment.

29. ***Teaching*** refers to communicating information with clarity and interest that helps people access knowledge and apply it to fulfill their own goals and plans.

30. ***Asserting*** refers to expressing goals, plans, and behaviors in a manner that demonstrates self-respect and respect for other people.

31. ***Self-Disclosing*** refers to communicating information about yourself in a manner that fosters openness with other people.

32. ***Respecting*** refers to being accepting, receptive, and courteous to other people.

33. ***Motivating*** refers to inspiring people to take action on goals and plans for higher levels of fulfillment.

34. ***Empowering*** refers to fostering self-responsibility and ability to accomplish goals and plans through assertive behavior that results in increased fulfillment.

35. ***Mediating*** refers to applying healthy communication skills to help other people get to the point where they can resolve their own disagreements and conflicts.

36. ***Counseling*** refers to applying communication skills to help people settle down and find in themselves how to fulfill their own goals and plans.

37. ***Parenting*** refers to applying communication skills to help children develop assertive balance in heart and mind to fulfill goals and plans.

38. ***Partnering*** refers to applying communication skills in a committed relationship to create deep, open communication that helps fulfill mutual goals and plans.

39. ***Integrating*** refers to fostering healthy coordination of heart, mind, body, and behavior for more open and deeper communication.

40. ***Unifying*** refers to connecting the individual soul or being with the underlying universal level of life, the universal Self or Being.

REFERENCES

[1]Boyer, R. W. (2008). *Bridge to unity: unified field-based science & spirituality*. Malibu, CA: Institute for Advanced Research.

[2]Maharishi Mahesh Yogi (1972). *Science of Creative Intelligence: Knowledge and Experience*. [33-lesson videotaped course]. Los Angeles, CA: MIU Press.

[3]O'Hanlon, W. & Weiner-Davis, M. (2003, 1989). *In search of solutions: A new direction in psychotherapy*. London: W. W. Norton and Co.

[4]Burns, D. D. (1990). *The feeling good handbook*. New York: Penguin.

[5]Fisher, R. & Ury, W. L. (1983). *Getting to yes*. New York: Penguin.

[6]McKay, M., Davis, M., & Fanning, P. (2003, 1983). *Messages: The communication skills book, 2nd Ed.* Oakland, CA: Harbinger Publications, Inc.

[7]Maharishi Mahesh Yogi (1963). *Science of Being and art of living*. Washington, DC: Age of Enlightenment Press.

[8]*Scientific Research on Maharishi's Transcendental Meditation and TM-Sidhi Program: Collected Papers, Vols. I-V*. (Various editors). Fairfield, IA: MUM Press.

ACKNOWLEDGEMENTS AND DEDICATION

I am grateful for the generous assistance and support of those who have given their wisdom, time, and energy to this work. It has been a work of love due to them.

I want to acknowledge fully the loving, patient, and wise contributions of my wife, Connie, who helped both the book and me become more practical and connected with the joys of daily life, and who also was the female voice on the audiobook. My beautiful stepdaughters, Heidi and Jenni, in their teens during development of the book, blessed us with many opportunities to apply the skills. I want to express deep appreciation to my parents, sister and family, as well as Connie's family, who honor me by their support, acceptance, and love.

Further, it is my pleasure to acknowledge the kind support and contributions of friends and colleagues who gave feedback to improve the book: J. Jarvis, Dr. D. Orme-Johnson, M. Spivak, P. Hensley, Dr. T. Olson-Sorflaten, Dr. D. Carter, Dr. P. Robertson, Dr. F. Travis, Dr. J. Wysong, Dr. K. Hutchinson, Drs. M. Dillbeck, Dr. S. Dillbeck, R. Moormeister, M. Zanger, M. Kincaid, M. Aguilar, M. Winters, E. Kaplan, and R. Barnett. Sincere thanks also to Allen Cobb, Liz Howard, and Denyce Rusch for helping with the editing, cover design, and publishing process. I want to give special thanks and recognition to Dr. D. E. Charleston and his son, Sean, for help with the non-verbal communication section, recording and preparing the audiobook, as well as for making the world a funnier place to live.

The deepest knowledge in this book—levels of mind and inner silence as the platform for healthy communication—come from the understanding of communication I developed through studying the science of consciousness of Vedic scientist and educator Maharishi Mahesh Yogi. I am honored to express appreciation by dedicating the book to him.

Finally, I want to express appreciation for each person who uses healthy communication skills to improve the quality of life for all of us. Thank you for applying the skills of how to communicate with body, mind, heart, and soul.

Made in the USA
Middletown, DE
16 January 2016